S320
INFECTIOUS DISEASE

1

PATHOGENS AND PEOPLE

prepared for the Course Team by
Basiro Davey, David Male and Michael Gillman

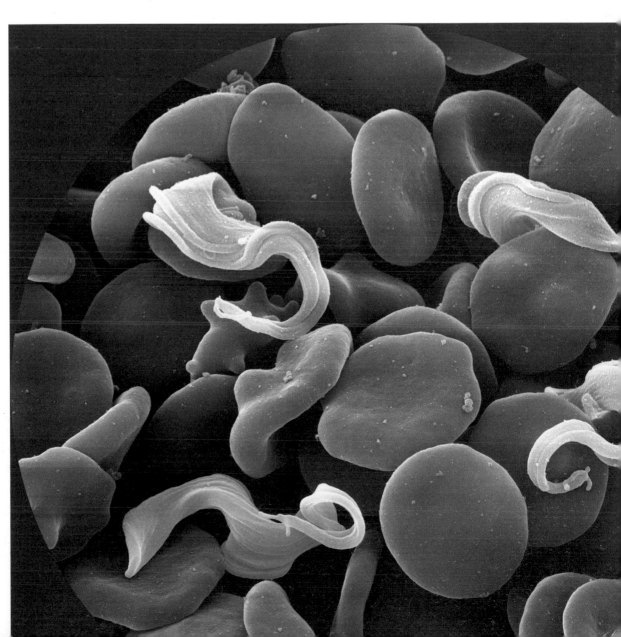

Cover picture: Coloured scanning electron micrograph of trypanosomes (*Trypanosoma brucei,* yellow). These protozoa are the cause of sleeping sickness. They are vector-borne parasites transmitted by the African blood- sucking tsetse fly (*Glossina sp.*). The life stage seen here (trypomastigotes) circulates in the bloodstream of the human host, dividing rapidly. The trypanosomes do not enter red blood cells (red) but can invade the cerebrospinal fluid and fatally damage the brain if the disease is left untreated.

This publication forms part of an Open University course [course code and title]. [The complete list of texts which make up this course can be found at the back (where applicable)]. Details of this and other Open University courses can be obtained from the Course Information and Advice Centre, PO Box 724, The Open University, Milton Keynes MK7 6ZS, United Kingdom: tel. +44 (0)1908 653231, e-mail general-enquiries@open.ac.uk

Alternatively, you may visit the Open University website at http://www.open.ac.uk where you can learn more about the wide range of courses and packs offered at all levels by The Open University.

To purchase a selection of Open University course materials visit the webshop at www.ouw.co.uk, or contact Open University Worldwide, Michael Young Building, Walton Hall, Milton Keynes MK7 6AA, United Kingdom for a brochure. tel. +44 (0)1908 858785; fax +44 (0)1908 858787; e-mail ouwenq@open.ac.uk

The Open University
Walton Hall, Milton Keynes
MK7 6AA

First published 2003.

Edited, designed and typeset by The Open University.

Printed and bound in the United Kingdom by The Alden Group, Oxford.

ISBN 0 7492 52308

1.1

THE S320 COURSE TEAM

Course Team Chair

Michael Gillman

Course Manager

Viki Burnage

Course Team Assistant

Dawn Partner

Course Team Authors

Basiro Davey (Books 1 & 7)

Tim Halliday (Book 5)

Paddy Farringdon (Book 6)

Mike Gillman (Books 1 & 5)

Hilary Macqueen (Books 2 & 4)

David Male (Books 1, 3 & 7)

Consultant Authors

Eric Bowers (Book 2)

Christine Heading (Book 7)

Laura Hibberts (Books 2 & 4)

Ralph Muller (Book 7)

Editors

Pat Forster

Gilly Riley

Margaret Swithenby

Academic Reader

Mary Manley

External Course Assessor

Bo Drasar

OU Graphic Design

Roger Courthold

Sian Lewis

Video Editing

Wilf Eynon

Michael Francis

CD-ROM Production

Greg Black

Phil Butcher

BBC Production

Martin Kemp

Rights Executive

Christine Brady

Picture Research

Lydia Eaton

Indexer

Jean Macqueen

Course Websites

Patrina Law

Louise Olney

Sue Dugher

3

CONTENTS

'Girl in White with Cherries' c. 1831. Oil on canvas
(42"×24"). Attributed to Micah Williams.

This portrait of an unknown girl was preserved in
the artist's family, who recalled that the child died
in a cholera epidemic and that her parents never
claimed the painting.

1 INFECTIOUS DISEASE: AN INTRODUCTION

Many cross-references are made in this chapter to later parts of the course, where you will find more extensive discussion of the topics introduced here. Several key terms that you will encounter often in S320 are defined, sometimes in text boxes to aid revision and to make it easier for you to 'skip' if they are already familiar from previous study. Section 1.5.3 discusses the various ways in which population data on disease and death are presented in the chapter, highlighting reasons for caution when making comparisons between different times and places. You should bear these points in mind when you interpret data elsewhere in the course, and especially when you locate data on infectious diseases in other sources, including the Internet.

1.1 A force in human history

Since the 1980s, infectious disease has re-emerged at the top of the global health agenda, shattering the optimism following World War II that modern medical interventions, such as antibiotic therapy and mass vaccination programmes, could eradicate deaths from infection. The new awareness of infection as a major threat to health centred on the AIDS pandemic (Box 1.1). Acquired immune deficiency syndrome had already claimed over 21 million lives by the start of 2001, including 4.5 million children. By that date new infections with HIV (the human immunodeficiency virus) in Sub-Saharan Africa had accelerated past 16 000 per day; in some regions over 25% of the adult population were already infected and average life expectancy at birth had fallen by more than 10 years. (You will learn about the biological aspects of HIV and AIDS in the case study in Book 3.) But AIDS was not the only apparently 'new' infection to threaten human health. Later in this chapter we review some other 'emerging' infectious diseases in the twenty-first century, which have risen in importance against the general downward trend globally in infection as a cause of death.

The impact of HIV/AIDS on the economies and hence the political stability of heavily affected countries is a major cause for international concern, and reminds us that an infectious disease still has the potential to alter the course of a nation's history. Past epidemics and the long-term impact of endemic diseases (Box 1.1) have been among the most potent forces shaping the current global distribution of population and cultures. Their influence can be seen in the balance of political and economic power in the modern world. To explain why, we must go back 10 000 years.

BOX 1.1 Pandemic, epidemic and endemic infectious diseases

An **epidemic** of an infectious disease occurs when a high proportion of a population is susceptible to infection with a particular infectious agent, and when the transmission rate between people is high. Large numbers of people are infected during a short period of time and numbers of new cases of the disease typically rise steeply before declining. A **pandemic** is an epidemic on a worldwide scale, for example, as occurred with influenza in 1919 and HIV/AIDS since the mid-1980s. **Endemic** infectious diseases are permanently present in a population, because there is always a sufficient reservoir of **susceptible** (i.e. capable of sustaining an infection) people. For example, the common cold viruses cause endemic infection in countries like the UK; malaria is an endemic disease in many parts of Africa.

1.1.1 Pastoralism and the origins of epidemic infections

The replacement of nomadic hunter-gatherer populations by largely settled communities subsisting on agriculture and the products of herded livestock (pastoralism) began around 8000 BC in a few scattered places in present-day Egypt, Iran, China, Mexico, the Andes and coastal West Africa. These practices spread very slowly across the Eurasian landmass, taking over 4000 years to reach parts of Western Europe. They can be considered the most important cultural transition in human history, for four reasons.

First, the ability to grow and store surplus food in defended settlements stoked the population explosion that followed the agricultural revolution wherever it spread. More mouths could be fed, but the varied hunter-gatherer diets were replaced by diets dominated by bulky carbohydrates from cereals and (later) root vegetables, which in at least some regions were of such poor nutritional quality that average height and longevity declined. Over thousands of years, large centres of population gradually became established, and the wealth generated by agriculture, pastoralism and trade led to the founding of all the great civilizations of the past: from the imperial dynasties of ancient Egypt, Greece, Rome and China, to the European colonization of other continents after Columbus landed in the Americas in AD 1492.

Second, the domestication of birds and mammals as sources of food, clothing, traction, transport, fertilizer and building materials resulted in the sustained exposure of humans to the infectious agents harboured by those species. Although turkeys, ducks and guinea pigs were domesticated in some parts of Central and South America, it was only in the Eurasian landmass and parts of Africa that large mammals were brought under human control. Genetic comparisons between infectious agents found in cattle, pigs, sheep, horses, dogs and poultry, and those that now exclusively infect humans, suggest that, over several thousand years, infections derived from domesticated species gradually adapted to human hosts. (In Book 5 you will learn more about the process by which an infectious agent can adapt to a new host.) The importance of these infectious diseases cannot be overstated: smallpox and diphtheria are caused by infectious agents that are thought to have originated in cattle, and so too may the measles virus, although it is also closely related to the virus that causes distemper in domestic dogs; the infectious agent of influenza, pertussis (whooping cough) and polio are probably derived from those of pigs and ducks; the common cold is caused by viruses similar to those that infect the respiratory tract of horses.

Some infectious agents have remained capable of reproducing both in domestic species and in humans, for example, the bacteria causing tuberculosis (TB) or brucellosis can be transmitted from cows to people in infected milk. Although in the developed world pulmonary TB (which affects the lungs) is now almost exclusively spread through person-to-person contact, this has been achieved by eradicating TB infection from cattle herds. (You will learn about the biology of TB and its different forms in a case study in Book 2.) Even in the UK, bacteria in poultry, eggs and meat cause at least 100 000 cases of diarrhoea each year, and around 400 deaths, and they exact a far greater toll in developing countries (as Section 1.5 describes). Parasites that depend on pastoralism are also a major health problem in developing countries, circulating between livestock and people (Figure 1.1). Other infectious diseases (e.g. typhus) became widespread in humans only when forest habitats were cleared for grazing and agriculture, and large populations came into close proximity for the first time with reservoirs of infectious agents that few had previously encountered.

FIGURE 1.1 Tsetse flies transmit the parasites (*Trypanosoma* species) that cause up to half a million cases of sleeping sickness in Africa annually, from reservoirs of infection in domestic cattle, goats and pigs, and from wild mammals. Here a technician collects tsetse flies for a World Health Organization research programme in Zimbabwe.

Of the 1415 species of infectious and parasitic organisms *currently* known to cause human diseases (Table 1.1), over 60% have already been identified as zoonoses, that is, caused by infectious agents that can be transmitted to humans by at least one other species of vertebrate under naturally occurring conditions (Box 1.2 overleaf). (The biology of these agents is the subject of Book 2.)

TABLE 1.1 Estimated numbers of infectious agents currently causing human diseases.

Type of infectious agent	Number	
bacteria	538	
fungi (including yeasts)	307	
viruses	215	
prions	2	
parasitic protoctists (single celled)	66	
parasitic invertebrates (helminths)	287	
Total	1415	
of which zoonoses	868	(61%)

BOX 1.2   Zoonoses and vector-borne diseases

The World Health Organization (WHO) defines a **zoonosis** as a disease caused by an infection that can be transmitted to humans by other vertebrates under naturally occurring conditions. Transmission may be by *direct* contact (e.g. the rabies virus, which infects 30 000 people in India each year, most via a dog bite); by *indirect* contact, from infected food, water or some other environmental agent (e.g. the helminth parasites, such as tapeworms and flukes that infest cattle, pigs and sheep, are mainly transmitted to humans by indirect routes); or via an arthropod *vector*, usually an insect. About one fifth of zoonoses are also **vector-borne diseases** requiring an invertebrate intermediary (e.g. yellow fever is caused by a virus transmitted from monkeys to humans by mosquitoes, resulting in at least 30 000 deaths annually in Africa and the Americas). Only 3% of zoonoses have their main reservoir of infection in humans, but 33% of zoonotic diseases can be passed on directly by an infected person to other people (Taylor *et al.*, 2001; e.g. the plague bacterium is transmitted from rodents to humans via infected fleas, but is also transmissible directly between people during epidemics of pneumonic plague, when the bacteria infect the lungs). In this course we have adopted the WHO definition of zoonoses, but you will sometimes find the term being used less precisely to include infections like HIV, which originated in non-human vertebrates but which have since adapted exclusively to infect human hosts. The WHO definition of a zoonosis *excludes* HIV because it can no longer infect primates. TB is technically a zoonosis (and is counted as such in Table 1.1) because the causative bacteria can still be transmitted between humans and cattle; but in some texts it may be excluded on the grounds that pulmonary TB is now primarily passed directly from person to person.

Third, the crowding of large numbers of people into enclosed settlements created the ideal conditions for infectious diseases to spread very rapidly through populations. Waste accumulates, polluting water sources and spreading water-borne infections such as cholera and 'crowd' diseases like typhoid; this latter can also be transmitted in food and by direct contact between people. Infections dispersed by droplets in the air (e.g. influenza, pneumonic plague, measles, pulmonary TB), or by contact with pustules (smallpox, bubonic plague), or transmitted by body lice (typhus), rapidly become epidemics in crowded 'face-to-face' societies. Vector-borne diseases (Box 1.2), such as malaria and yellow fever, extend their range because their vectors can breed in irrigation ditches, paddy fields (Figure 1.2) and ponds created to water livestock. Vermin attracted to stored food carry fleas and lice that bring plague and typhus. The **infant mortality rate** (the number of deaths in the first year of life, per 1000 live births) in the South of England in the seventeenth century gives some indication of the death toll from infection in crowded towns and villages. Depending on the location, between 100 and 300 infants per 1000 born alive did not survive to their first birthday (Dobson, 1989), almost all dying from infectious diseases, often exacerbated by malnutrition.

Fourth, the acquisition of wealth in urban societies fuelled trade and political ambitions for foreign territory, spreading infections to new locations along trade routes and with expeditionary forces, and bringing back 'new' infections from far afield. An infectious disease in a new location can rapidly flare into an epidemic in a

FIGURE 1.2
The flooding of fields to create rice paddies creates ideal breeding grounds for the mosquitoes that transmit malarial parasites (*Plasmodium* species), and for the snails that act as intermediate hosts for human blood flukes (*Schistosoma* species).

'naïve' population in which everyone is susceptible. For example, between 1346 and 1350 Europe lost 20 million people to bubonic plague (the Black Death) – over 25% of its population – as rats, other rodents and their fleas spread the plague bacteria along trade routes from China to the English fens. Over time, epidemic infections either disappear altogether (as plague did in England after 1665) or become endemic (Box 1.1) – no longer 'new' in that location, but an ever-present threat to health, particularly among the young.

○ Explain why the young are most at risk from an endemic infection and how they contribute to maintaining the disease as endemic in a population.

● The survivors of infection develop some immunity to it, which enables them to resist further episodes; (the mechanisms underlying immunity to infection are the subject of Book 3). But people who have not encountered it before have no immunity. The proportion of 'susceptibles' in the population is reduced by deaths, but is continually topped up by births (and also by immigration from areas where the infection is not endemic), creating a pool of mainly young individuals in whom the disease is sustained.

However, even though the disease remains endemic, the **case fatality rate** of a particular infection (the proportion of infected individuals who die) tends to fall gradually in a population, over many generations.

○ Use the theory of evolution by natural selection to explain why this occurs, referring to the inherent genetic variation in susceptibility to the infection that exists between individuals in a susceptible population.

● During an epidemic, the 'most resistant' individuals survive to produce more children in the next generation than the 'least resistant', thereby passing on more copies of the genetic traits for infection resistance. Over many generations spanning perhaps hundreds of years, the proportion of the population that can survive the infection will increase (i.e. the case fatality rate falls).

History tells us that this downward trend is often punctuated by a resurgence of deaths as a new epidemic of the infection breaks out. The reason may be because the infectious agent has undergone a genetic change, which results in greater **virulence** – the ability to establish an infection – or because a larger population of susceptible individuals is available, for example during population migrations or surges in the birth rate. Thus a cycle tends to become established in which the impact of an infection on a population fluctuates over periods of decline and resurgence in a relatively stable pattern, until human actions alter the balance.

For example, HIV was probably endemic in a few rural African populations for decades before it spread to a city and the rest of the world via multiple routes: heterosexual and homosexual intercourse, drug injecting, infected blood products and transfusions, and from mother to child. Thus the AIDS pandemic can be viewed as partly a consequence of modern air travel and tourism, and partly the circumstances that drive people into sex work or drug injecting, as well as to the biology of the virus. Turn the clock further back, and the social divisions of wealth and entitlement that emerged in urban civilizations founded on the profits of agriculture and pastoralism can be seen to underlie the present unequal distribution of HIV (and most other diseases and disabilities) among the most disadvantaged members of modern societies.

1.1.2 Pestilence and empires

The gradual adaptation of agricultural and pastoral populations in Europe to become more resistant to the infectious agents derived from those of their domesticated animals had a profound influence on the rest of the world. We have not the space here to embark on a history of human epidemics and their impact on empires and nationhood (see *Further sources* at the end of this book if you wish to read further). However, we can illustrate the general claim that the course of human history has been profoundly influenced by infectious diseases transported from a part of the world where they had become endemic, to regions where the entire population was susceptible.

For example, Athens faded as the epicentre of ancient Greece when an unknown epidemic swept in from North Africa in 430 BC with troops returning from campaigns, killing more than a quarter of the population in three years. The decline of one civilization assisted the rise of another – ancient Rome – which had even greater ambitions to colonize distant lands. Between AD 165–180 five million people died from smallpox brought back from Asia by the army, killing a quarter of the Roman population; a smallpox epidemic in Rome in the second century AD resulted in 5000 deaths a day. The huge and sustained mortality from malaria is given prime place by historians in the fall of the Roman Empire; it was exacerbated by the first plague pandemic, beginning in AD 540, which spread right across Europe. Plague killed over 40% of the population of Constantinople (Istanbul since 1453) in this outbreak, a proportion that exceeded even the medieval pandemic of the Black Death mentioned above.

The link between pestilence and empire-building is also evident in the European colonization of the Americas, particularly in the seventeenth century. The indigenous peoples whose lands were appropriated still lived either as hunter-gatherers or as arable farmers who did not herd livestock, whereas more than 5000 years of co-existence had already taken place between European colonists and the infections derived from their domestic animals.

○ Why is this different history significant?

● The colonists came from populations in which some resistance had evolved to infectious diseases originating in pastoral species, because many of the less resistant humans had died in successive epidemics. The indigenous peoples had no previous contact with these infections, so the entire population was susceptible to them.

Within 100 years of Columbus landing in Hispaniola in 1492, the indigenous population of the American continent north of Mexico had fallen from an estimated 10 million to under 2 million, wiped out by 'European' diseases. The tiny expeditionary forces to Central and South America begun by Cortés (1519) and Pizarro (1531) destroyed the Aztec and Inca civilizations of Mexico and Peru, in large measure due to the import of smallpox and measles. The Aztec capital was the second largest city in the world at that date (exceeded in size only by Istanbul) and had housed 300 000 people, half of whom died from smallpox in the three months that Cortés laid siege to the city. With each successive wave of colonization, the importation of domesticated livestock from Europe accelerated the disease toll on indigenous populations. Measles, influenza and typhus killed two million in Mexico in about 1600. A similar fate met the native peoples of the Canary Islands, Australasia and the Pacific archipelago within a few years of European colonization. Since these societies had never domesticated large mammals, they had very little by way of 'novel' infections to exchange for the diseases that destroyed them – only syphilis may have made the return journey to Europe in the first period of colonization. (The TV programme associated with this course, *In Search of Syphilis*, considers the origins of syphilis in Britain.)

In the seventeenth century, which was the main period of migration from Britain to North America, settlers brought malaria to the 'new world' from the marshlands of Kent, where the protoctist parasite *Plasmodium vivax* was endemic, and it rapidly spread south from the tidal regions of New England. Deaths from malaria soared in the late seventeenth century when a more virulent parasite, *Plasmodium falciparum*, was imported to the Americas from Africa with the slave trade. (Malaria is the subject of the case study in Chapter 3 of this book.) A total of over 20 million African slaves were transported to replace the 'workforce' of indigenous peoples destroyed by the colonists. They also brought yellow fever and leprosy, to which they had greater resistance than the white settlers, while the slaves themselves died mainly from influenza, pneumonia and TB. The colonization of the Americas illustrates the speed at which the endemic infectious diseases of one region can 'globalize' along routes of population migration and trade (see Dobson, 1989 for a detailed account).

The exploitation of the Indian sub-continent in the late eighteenth and early nineteenth centuries offers further examples. The military conquest of territory from the Ganges delta in the east to the western seaboard established vast colonial plantations and spread malaria and cholera from pockets of endemic disease throughout the continent. *Vibrio cholerae*, the bacteria that cause cholera, live in streams, lakes and marine estuaries. When people are infected they develop copious watery diarrhoea, and as armies and traders moved across India, they contaminated water sources with the bacteria. Population displacement spread the disease still further, until cholera became endemic throughout the sub-continent and was transported to Europe and as far as Japan. Cholera may have first reached Europe some 200 years earlier, but the expanding trade with India fuelled the pandemics of

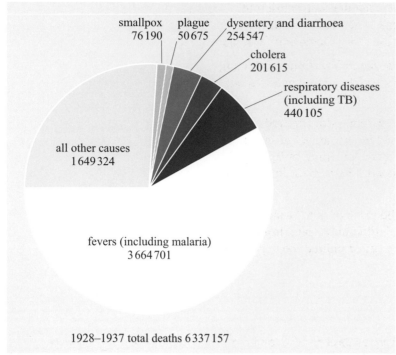

smallpox
76 190

plague
50 675

dysentery and diarrhoea
254 547

cholera
201 615

respiratory diseases
(including TB)
440 105

all other causes
1 649 324

fevers (including malaria)
3 664 701

1928–1937 total deaths 6 337 157

FIGURE 1.3
Proportional mortality by cause for over 6 million deaths between 1928 and 1937 in regions of India under British rule. This method of representing mortality data uses a 'pie chart' with segments corresponding to the proportion of deaths due to each cause; the final section of this chapter discusses the interpretation of

the nineteenth century. About 7000 people died from cholera in London alone in 1832, the same year that cholera arrived on trade ships in North America. Between 1847 and 1861 over 2.5 million Russians were infected and more than 1 million died. (The biology of cholera is the subject of a case study in Book 2.) Even in the first half of the twentieth century, death rates from infectious epidemics still occurred on a huge scale in the colonial territories of European powers (see, for example, Figure 1.3). Plague killed 12 million Indians between 1900–1950.

Infectious diseases have also impacted on empires by influencing the outcome of warfare. Until the twentieth century, more soldiers died from infectious disease during military campaigns than from battle wounds. For example, the deaths of 30 000 soldiers from typhus in 1542 cut short the Holy Roman Empire's assault on the Ottomans; in 1802, the same disease destroyed half a million men and halted Napoleon's invasion of Russia. In the American Civil War (1861–1865), dysentery and typhoid accounted for most of the 186 000 deaths from infectious disease on the Union side – twice as many as died in the fighting. In the Boer War (1899–1902), fought by Britain against Dutch settlers in South Africa, the British army's defeat was due primarily to the loss of 13 000 soldiers to typhoid – 5000 more than were killed in action. Without exception, wars also spread infection among non-combatants caught up in the conflict. The next chapter in this book is a case study of influenza, which reached pandemic levels in 1919 and caused 20 million deaths worldwide, a greater number than died in World War I. This war also spread an epidemic of typhus in Russia, which killed three million people and affected 25 million more between 1914 and 1921, delaying the establishment of a stable socialist state until after the 1917 revolution.

Viewed against the devastating effects of infectious disease in such recent past history, it seems remarkable that the middle of the twentieth century was a period of widespread optimism in Western industrialized nations that infection could be 'defeated'. But beyond the battlefield and the population displacement it caused, a steady decline in deaths from infection had been occurring in countries such as Britain since the early nineteenth century. It is to these signs of success that we turn next.

Summary of Section 1.1

1   Infectious disease has been affecting the course of human history, the distribution of populations and the rise and fall of empires, colonies, armies and political powers from antiquity to the present day.

2   The domestication of large mammals and poultry in the Eurasian continent from about 8000 BC initiated the gradual adaptation of infectious agents from these species to survival in human hosts, resulting in major epidemic and pandemic disease outbreaks with huge loss of human life in susceptible populations.

3   Large settled communities created conditions favouring the transmission of infection between individuals and across continents while trading with each other, disputing territory in warfare, and clearing land for grazing and farming.

4   Over many generations, European populations exposed to infections originating in domestic species evolved some resistance to them. This resistance was not shared by the indigenous peoples whose lands they colonized.

5   The economic and political disadvantage suffered by countries referred to as 'developing' today has, at least in part, been shaped by the impact of infectious diseases introduced in the colonial period, either by the colonists or by the transportation of African slaves, and which destroyed several great indigenous civilizations of the past.

6   Of the infectious diseases currently identified in humans, over 60% are zoonoses (i.e. caused by infectious agents transmissible to humans from reservoirs in other vertebrate animals, either by direct or indirect contact, or by arthropod vectors).

1.2 Past success

One can think of the middle of the twentieth century as the end of one of the most important social revolutions in history, the virtual elimination of the infectious disease as a significant factor in social life.

(Burnet, 1962)

From the perspective of a new millennium, the failure of this prediction is all too obvious. But in 1962, Macfarlane Burnet's confidence in the power of medical science was understandable. His assertion was made in the aftermath of his Nobel Prize, shared with Peter Medawar in 1960, for research that laid the foundations of modern **immunology** (the scientific study of the immune system and its response to infection; the subject of Book 3 of this course). Burnet had described the processes underlying the acquisition of **immunity** – the resistance to subsequent infection with a particular infectious agent, which develops naturally in humans and most other vertebrates after the first exposure. His work advanced the expectation that vaccination with 'safe' extracts of infectious agents would, in time, abolish human infectious disease.

Burnet's optimism was widely shared by the scientific and medical community of the period and by Western governments, who had already seen remarkable progress in the decline of fatal infections in advanced industrial nations (e.g. in the USA, Figure 1.4 overleaf). The only infection to inflict massive mortality in these nations in the twentieth century was the 1919 influenza pandemic, which killed 500 000 in the USA alone; its temporary impact on the downward trend in infection is apparent in Figure 1.4. The effects of HIV in wealthy countries since the 1980s have not (yet) approached this scale.

In 1900, the leading causes of mortality in Western Europe and the USA were pneumonia and other respiratory infections, pulmonary TB, typhoid, and infections that disproportionately killed young children: whooping cough, measles, diarrhoea, diphtheria and scarlet fever. Taken together, infectious diseases accounted for over 40% of deaths. Table 1.2 (overleaf) shows data for Scotland in 1900, underlining the point made earlier about the susceptibility of the young to endemic infections,

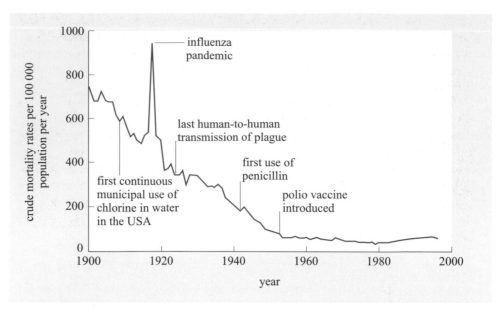

FIGURE 1.4

Trends in infectious disease mortality (crude mortality rates per 100 000 population per year), USA, 1900–1996. The meaning of 'crude' mortality rates is discussed in Section 1.5.3.

which killed over 15 000 children aged under five in that year. The infant mortality rate in Scotland in 1900 was 129 deaths in the first year of life per 1000 live births. A century later, the expectation of life at birth had risen by over 30 years, with around three-quarters of the gain due to the decline in mortality from infectious disease. In Scotland in 2001 there were 41 deaths from infection in children aged under five years, and the infant mortality rate had fallen to around 6 deaths per 1000 live births. The leading causes of mortality in developed countries had become heart disease, strokes and cancers, and the proportion due to infection had fallen to under 15%, of which all but 0.5% was due to respiratory infections, mainly in older people. In Section 1.5.2 we briefly review the current main causes of infectious disease in the UK.

TABLE 1.2 Deaths in 1900 from the leading infectious diseases in Scotland, all ages combined and children aged under 5 years.

Infectious disease	Deaths, all ages combined	Deaths under 5 years (and as % of all deaths from that cause)	
respiratory diseases (not TB)	15 674	6242	(40%)
tuberculosis (all forms)	10 509	2535	(24%)
diarrhoea	2509	2013	(80%)
whooping cough	1736	1662	(96%)
measles	1770	1618	(91%)
diphtheria	783	582	(74%)
scarlet fever	634	420	(66%)
typhoid/enteric fever	603	26	(4%)
smallpox	56	14	(25%)
typhus	34	1	(3%)
Total deaths from leading infections	34 308	15 113	
deaths from these infections as % of all deaths	43%	not available	

Most of the decline in infectious disease in Western Europe and the USA up to the end of World War II was not due to medical interventions but to improvements in the standard of living, nutritional quality and domestic and personal hygiene, and to **public health strategies**. These latter aimed to improve the health of the whole population, for example by introducing legislation to govern sanitation and water purity, housing standards and food safety. Two illustrations of the general trend appear in Figures 1.5 and 1.6: the huge reduction in deaths from TB in Britain and the reduction in child deaths from whooping cough in Scotland both occurred long before effective medical treatment and vaccination became available. The continuing importance of public health strategies to prevent infection or contain its spread, for example through water purification, sexual health education, contact tracing and isolation of infectious 'cases', and swift identification of sources of contamination (e.g. as is routine in the catering industry), is illustrated in many parts of this course, but particularly in the final book.

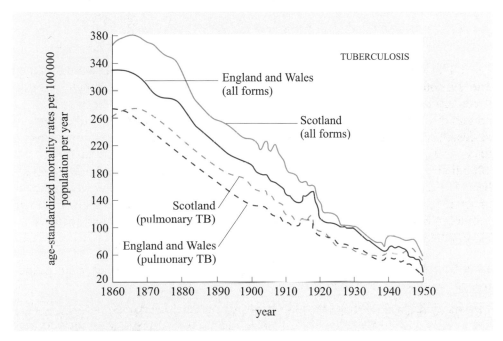

FIGURE 1.5
Age-standardized death rates from all forms of TB per 100 000 population, England and Wales, and Scotland, 1860–1950. There were about 100 000 deaths annually in the mid-nineteenth century. Treatment with streptomycin began in 1947; vaccination became widespread from 1954. Age standardization is discussed in Section 1.5.3.

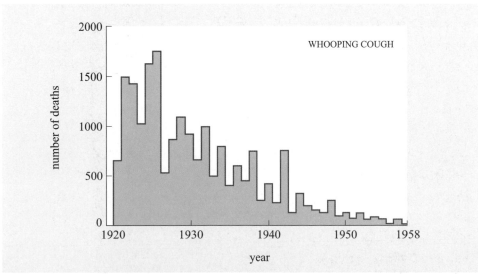

FIGURE 1.6
Deaths from whooping cough, Scotland 1920–1958. Treatment with sulphonamides began about 1940; vaccination was introduced from 1950. The use of 'raw numbers' of deaths, rather than death *rates*, is discussed in Section 1.5.3.

While acknowledging that public health measures had contributed to the rapid decline in infectious disease in countries like the UK and USA, by the late 1950s medical scientists such as Burnet were placing their confidence in therapeutic advances and new vaccines to eradicate infection altogether. By the end of the twentieth century, vaccination had become the major strategy for controlling the potentially fatal infectious diseases of childhood. Over 90% of children in Western countries like the UK are protected against many of the major **vaccine-preventable diseases**: diphtheria, whooping cough (pertussis), tetanus, measles, mumps, rubella, polio and TB.

Moreover, it was expected that medical strategies would bring to Africa, Asia and Latin America the progress in health already seen in the advanced industrial economies. The expectation of life at birth in these regions had also been on a rising trend throughout the twentieth century, but the problems of introducing a safe water supply and sanitation throughout the developing world were and remain immense, both in terms of the financial cost and the technical difficulties (for example, sewers cannot be dug in mountains, deserts and many other locations). Thus medical intervention was expected to deliver what public health strategies could not provide, and at little cost to the richer nations.

In the 1950s, a vigorous international effort began to tackle the endemic infectious diseases of the developing world with new drugs like the sulphonamides and antibiotics, with insecticides (particularly DDT) to reduce mosquitoes and other insect vectors of infection, and by numerous vaccination programmes. In 1958, the WHO was formed as an agency of the United Nations, and tackling infectious disease was put at the top of its agenda. In 1975 it committed member states to deliver 'Health for All by the Year 2000' by a resolution known as the Alma Ata Declaration. In May 1980, the WHO declared the world free from smallpox – the first successful campaign to eradicate a major infectious disease, which had once killed millions worldwide. Other successes were expected to follow, and indeed great progress has been made towards the global elimination of polio (the subject of a case study on vaccination in the final book of this course).

However, the optimism of those times has faded. Just two years after the official announcement that smallpox was no longer a threat, the first cases of AIDS were identified in the USA.

Summary of Section 1.2

1   At the start of the twentieth century, infectious diseases accounted for around 40% of all deaths in Western industrial countries, disproportionately affecting children aged under 5 years – a situation mirrored in developing countries today.

2   By the end of the twentieth century, deaths from infection in the developed world had fallen to around 15% of all deaths, and life expectancy at birth had risen by around 30 years. Advances also occurred in developing countries, but at a much slower pace.

3   Most of the decline in infectious disease before 1950 was due to rising living standards, increased personal hygiene and public health strategies, accelerated after 1950 by mass vaccination programmes and new drug treatments.

4   In 1958, the WHO put tackling infectious disease in developing countries at the top of the health agenda with some success, culminating in the global

eradication of smallpox in 1980. The trend continues downwards for most infectious diseases, but the start of the HIV/AIDS pandemic in about 1982 quenched earlier optimism that all infectious disease could be eradicated.

1.3 Categorizing infection

In Sections 1.4 and 1.5 we present a brief review of contemporary infectious disease patterns. But first we must introduce some key terms and concepts.

1.3.1 Pathogens, parasites and hosts

So far in this chapter, we have used the term infectious 'agents' to avoid problems inherent in other collective nouns, but we cannot avoid unpacking them any longer. Apart from certain stages in the development of parasitic invertebrates, such as tapeworms and flukes, most infectious agents are too small to see with the naked eye, and are often referred to as **microbes** or microorganisms because they can only be viewed with a microscope. Viruses and prions (infectious proteins) are not living cells and so cannot be 'organisms', but are nevertheless included under this umbrella term. However, only a tiny fraction of all the microbes that exist cause infectious disease, so an alternative term for those that do is **pathogen** (from *pathogenic*, disease causing). This usage is problematic too, since the large invertebrate parasites are also 'pathogenic', but it enables us to make a distinction that is sometimes useful.

Another problem relates to the term **parasite**, which in everyday language is applied only to the invertebrate animals (such as fleas, lice, *helminth* worms and flukes) and to single-celled parasites (pathogenic *protoctists*) that live in or on the body of a larger organism (their **host**), deriving a benefit from this arrangement and causing harm to the host. (Book 2 will explain the biology of helminths and protoctist parasites.) In S320, we have elected to follow the everyday usage and restrict 'parasite' to the invertebrates and single-celled parasites that cause human disease. However, you should be aware that strictly speaking, in biological terms, *all* the pathogenic microbes that live in or on a host can also be called 'parasites' (since they derive a benefit from and harm their host). Many scientific sources outside this course use 'parasite' in this all-encompassing sense, and further discussion of parasitism as a way of life occurs in Book 2, Chapter 1.

You should also be aware that for simplicity we have generally used **infectious disease** as a collective term for all diseases caused by pathogens *and* parasites. This usage is widespread, except among scientists and doctors who specialize exclusively in *parasitic diseases*, a term you will encounter in the chapter on invertebrate parasites in Book 2.

Finally, it is important to recognize from the outset that the occurrence and progress of an infectious disease is as much a consequence of processes in the *host* as it is due to the action of the infectious agent, and *both* are influenced by external factors such as the proportion of 'susceptibles' in the population, and many other things. Although we repeatedly refer to a pathogen or parasite as *causing* a disease, the factors that contribute to its **aetiology** (underlying causes) are multiple and interacting.

◻ What host factors might contribute to the aetiology of a food-borne diarrhoeal disease in a specific individual?

⬤ The person's genetic makeup will exert an influence on susceptibility or resistance to infection by that agent; general health, nutritional status and exposure to stress are among many factors that could affect the competence of his or her immune response to infection (although the evidence is equivocal, except under extreme circumstances such as starvation). You may also have thought of behavioural factors: poor hygiene during food preparation and inadequate cooking of raw ingredients may be the most important 'cause' of the illness. If you expand your vision even further, you might conclude that poverty, poor education and lack of adequate sanitation underlie the inability of this person to acquire food that is safe to eat.

In Book 5, we examine **host–pathogen interactions** in some detail, and rather than seeing them as opponents in a war, we focus on evidence that their relationship *co-evolves* over time, each adapting to the other.

1.3.2 Categories of infectious disease

There are many overlapping ways in which infectious diseases are commonly categorized, as summarized in Table 1.3.

◻ Suggest a specific example of an infectious disease in each category (a)–(h).

TABLE 1.3 Common categorizations for human infectious diseases.

Categorization criterion	Descriptive terms	Specific examples
type of infectious agent	bacterial, viral, fungal or prion infections; parasitic diseases	(a)
transmission to humans via insects or other invertebrates (e.g. snails)	vector-borne diseases	(b)
horizontal transmission between people via indirect contact	food-borne, water-borne or airborne diseases	(c)
horizontal transmission between people via direct contact	wound infections; sexually transmitted infections	(d)
vertical transmission from mother to baby in pregnancy or birth	materno–fetal infections	(e)
symptoms	e.g. diarrhoeal diseases; fevers; rashes, pustules and 'spots'	(f)
part of the body affected	e.g. respiratory infections; gastrointestinal infections	(g)
transmissible to humans by other vertebrates	zoonoses	(h)

● There are many other examples in addition to those that follow, all of which have been mentioned earlier in the chapter, or will be familiar from general knowledge: (a) TB is caused by a bacterial infection, polio is viral, thrush is fungal, variant Creutzfeldt-Jakob disease (vCJD) is caused by prions, and sleeping sickness is a parasitic disease; (b) malaria, typhus and sleeping sickness are vector-borne diseases transmitted by (respectively) mosquitoes, body lice and tsetse flies; (c) salmonella poisoning is food-borne, cholera mainly water-borne, and measles and influenza are airborne infections; (d) HIV and syphilis are sexually transmitted infections (STIs); (e) HIV and syphilis can also be vertically transmitted; (f) cholera causes diarrhoea; malaria, diphtheria, whooping cough and scarlet fever all cause high temperatures (fever); 'spots' of various types characterize smallpox, bubonic plague, measles and chickenpox; (g) influenza is a respiratory infection and cholera is a gastrointestinal infection; (h) yellow fever, sleeping sickness, TB and rabies are zoonoses.

Categories (c), (d) and (e) in Table 1.3 are often referred to collectively as **communicable diseases** because the infectious agents are transmitted from person to person, even if indirectly via food, water or air. The pathogens responsible for **non-communicable diseases** cannot be 'caught' from another person; they include the vector-borne diseases and many other infections, for example tetanus and legionella (Legionnaire's disease). Two thirds of zoonoses are non-communicable, TB being the most notable exception.

Infectious diseases can also be categorized according to the *timescale* of the illness. An **acute infection** is one that produces disease symptoms that either kill the host or resolve quickly (within days or weeks). When it subsides, this is usually because the pathogen that caused it has been completely eliminated from the body by the host's immune response (for example, influenza symptoms resolve when the virus has been eradicated); in such cases, the host is said to have developed a **sterile immunity** to that pathogen. However, some pathogens are not eliminated, but become hidden and cause a **latent infection** that persists within the body, but without producing symptoms. For example, after recovery from chickenpox, the herpes zoster virus can remain latent in nerve cells and reactivate years later to cause shingles.

A **chronic infection** occurs when the immune system fails to eliminate the infectious agent, which continues to produce disease symptoms and tissue damage over many months or years; for example, *Mycobacterium tuberculosis* causes chronic TB. Parasites generally cause chronic disease, but acute 'crises' can also occur when the underlying infection flares up again, as for example in sleeping sickness or malaria.

Throughout this course, you will meet all these categorizations and you should be aware that any infectious disease can simultaneously be a member of more than one category. For example, Chapters 2–4 present three case studies: on influenza (an acute viral respiratory infection); malaria (a vector-borne chronic parasitic infection of the bloodstream, causing intermittent fever); and hospital acquired infections (most are bacterial infections of surgical wounds, or bloodstream infections, but some produce respiratory or diarrhoeal diseases, and some are caused by viruses or fungi).

Summary of Section 1.3

1 Disease-causing infectious agents are commonly distinguished as either pathogens (pathogenic bacteria, viruses, fungi and prions), or as parasites, which include certain single-celled protoctists and invertebrate animals (mainly helminths).

2 The underlying causes of an infectious disease encompass not only the infectious agent involved, but also factors in the host and in the environment.

3 Infectious diseases can be categorized in terms of the causative infectious agent, the symptoms, duration or site of infection, and the route of transmission. Zoonoses are caused by infectious agents that can be transmitted to humans by other vertebrates under naturally occurring conditions.

1.4 The re-emergence of infectious disease

1.4.1 Unusual disease outbreaks

We can now return to the historical narrative that we left at the end of Section 1.2. In the 1980s, the AIDS pandemic shattered confidence in the ability of medicine to eradicate infectious disease. Other worrying signs followed, many of which will be familiar to you from coverage in the media.

○ Summarize the main reasons for increasing concern about threats from infectious disease since the 1980s (excluding HIV/AIDS). Try to illustrate each reason with a specific disease example, and then compare your notes with ours. (We have added details you may not have recalled, but you should recognize most categories in the list.)

■ 1 Rates of some 'old enemies' began to rise again after a period of decline, or the rate of increase accelerated: TB in developing countries in the wake of HIV, and in Western nations among disadvantaged groups; plague in parts of Africa, Madagascar, Brazil, Peru and Viet Nam; cholera in South America; sleeping sickness in Central Africa; and dengue fever in tropical regions around the world.

2 Previously unknown pathogens caused outbreaks of new diseases: Ebola virus was identified as the cause of a fatal haemorrhagic fever in Africa; Hantavirus pulmonary syndrome emerged in South America and rapidly spread to South East Asia and the USA; Nipah virus was discovered as the source of a fatal 'flu-like illness in Malaysia; the prion disease vCJD was first identified in Britain. A new virus, hepatitis C (HCV), was identified in 1989 as the cause of previously unattributable chronic liver disease, not caused by the well known hepatitis B virus (HBV); by 1999, HCV was estimated to have infected 140 million people worldwide, with 3 to 4 million new infections occurring annually.

3 Endemic infections previously confined to particular regions of the world suddenly appeared in other continents: Japanese encephalitis virus spread to Australia, possibly in aircraft-borne or wind-blown mosquitoes; West Nile virus appeared in Eastern Europe, North Africa, Italy, France and the USA; Rift Valley fever spread to Saudi Arabia and Yemen; cholera returned to South America in 1991 for the first time in over a century.

4 More virulent strains of known infections were isolated: the food-borne bacterium *Escherichia coli* (*E. coli*) strain O157 caused bloody diarrhoea and some deaths in outbreaks in Europe, the USA, Japan and Africa; in European children it became the commonest cause of kidney damage severe enough to require a transplant. Influenza virus strain H5N1 caused an epidemic in Hong Kong. The proportion of tropical dengue virus cases that involved severe haemorrhage rose swiftly in South East Asia and the Americas.

5 The diagnosis of some common infections began to rise, particularly food-borne infections, which reached 33 million episodes annually in the USA and caused 900 deaths. Sexually transmitted infections other than HIV also increased; particular concern was expressed about infertility due to *Chlamydia*, which doubled its infection rate in the UK between 1995 and 2000 to 1 in 100 teenage girls. (In Section 1.5.3 we refer to the problem of distinguishing between a genuine rise in infection rates and improved *detection* rates.)

6 Increasing numbers of drug-resistant strains of bacteria, including those causing TB and surgical wound infections, were identified, raising fears that these conditions could become untreatable. Hopes for curing HIV faded when drug-resistant strains of the virus rapidly evolved. Drug-resistance in African *Trypanosoma* parasites was shown to underlie the resurgence of sleeping sickness.

7 The threat to human lives and livelihoods from infectious diseases in farm animals was demonstrated by the slaughter of half the pigs in Malaysia in 1999 in an attempt to control an epidemic of Nipah virus encephalitis; 3.3 million sheep and half a million cattle were destroyed in the UK epidemic of foot and mouth disease in 2001; both diseases were caused by picornaviruses.

8 Finally, the terrorist attacks on the USA in September 2001 spread panic about the possibility of 'biological terrorists' disseminating pathogens and causing diseases such as anthrax and smallpox in civilian populations.

These trends began to be researched and discussed under the umbrella title of **emerging infectious diseases** (EIDs), defined as new, re-emerging or drug-resistant infections, which have increased significantly in humans in the past two decades, or which threaten to increase in the future. Of the infectious agents numbered in Table 1.1 (p. 9), a total of 175 (12%) were involved in EIDs. On the principle that 'accurate intelligence is the best defence', surveillance data on morbidity and mortality from these EIDs were pooled by national disease registries around the world (e.g. the Centers for Disease Control and Prevention (CDC) in the USA and the Public Health Laboratory Service (PHLS) in the UK); notifiable diseases were reported to the WHO (see Box 1.3 overleaf). The Internet websites of the CDC, PHLS and WHO are among the most extensive and accessible sources of surveillance data on infectious diseases nationally and globally, and are listed under *Further Sources* at the end of this book and in the *Resources* section of the course website.

The WHO established 'EID rapid response teams' which aim to arrive at EID outbreaks anywhere in the world within 24 hours of notification (Figure 1.7 overleaf), and it has taken the lead in promoting research to establish the underlying causes of EIDs – to which we now turn.

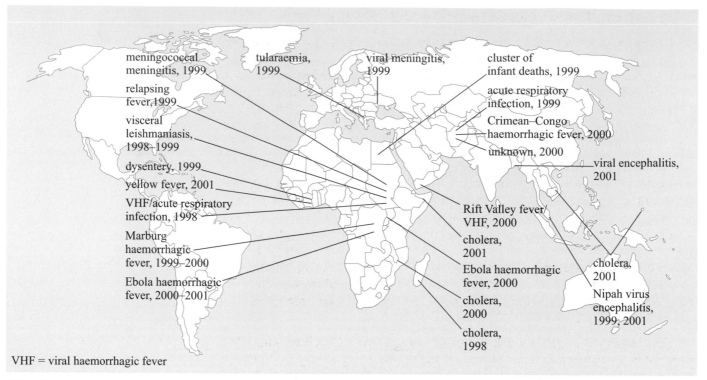

meningococcal meningitis, 1999

tularaemia, 1999

viral meningitis, 1999

cluster of infant deaths, 1999

relapsing fever, 1999

acute respiratory infection, 1999

visceral leishmaniasis, 1998–1999

Crimean–Congo haemorrhagic fever, 2000

dysentery, 1999

unknown, 2000

yellow fever, 2001

viral encephalitis, 2001

VHF/acute respiratory infection, 1998

Rift Valley fever/VHF, 2000

Marburg haemorrhagic fever, 1999–2000

cholera, 2001

Ebola haemorrhagic fever, 2000

cholera, 2001

Ebola haemorrhagic fever, 2000–2001

Nipah virus encephalitis, 1999, 2001

cholera, 2000

cholera, 1998

VHF = viral haemorrhagic fever

FIGURE 1.7   Some WHO-facilitated 'rapid response' missions to epidemics of emerging infectious diseases around the world, 1998–2001.

BOX 1.3   Surveillance data, notifiable diseases, morbidity and mortality

Every country in the world collects disease **surveillance data** on the number of episodes of specified diseases, disorders or disabilities (**morbidity**) and on the number of deaths from specific causes (**mortality**). The age and sex of each 'case' may also be noted in a central registry. However, methods of collecting and reporting these data may be inadequate in developing countries; even in the UK (which established the world's first disease registry in the nineteenth century) there is some unreliability due to incomplete or inaccurate reporting. The most important diseases are often made legally **notifiable**: in 2000 there were 58 notifiable infectious diseases in the USA. Morbidity and mortality *estimates* can help to increase the accuracy of surveillance data by collecting information from a defined population sample. For example, an important UK source is the 'weekly returns service' from a large sample of family doctors reporting all cases seen that week to the Royal College of General Practitioners (later in the chapter we present data from this source in Figure 1.10 and Table 1.4). Survey data are then extrapolated to give an estimate for the population as a whole. National surveillance data on certain diseases of global importance are reported to the WHO, which tracks long-term trends.

1.4.2 Infection and culture: a dynamic exchange

The factors contributing to the pattern of emerging infectious diseases are complex and interacting, as Section 1.1 illustrated. Such patterns demonstrate the *dynamic* nature of the relationship between pathogens, humans and other animals, the natural and built environment, social organization and cultural practices, new technology and trade, political systems and ideologies. Disturbances to the balance between these factors can precipitate sudden epidemics, drive the evolution of drug-resistant strains, and transport infectious diseases around the world.

A major factor has undoubtedly been the huge increase in air travel and inter-continental tourism, which has contributed to the globalization of HIV and TB, and sporadically brings rare diseases into susceptible populations (e.g. the import to Europe of Lassa fever from Africa and hantavirus pulmonary syndrome from South America). Warfare, population dispersal, economic migration and mass pilgrimage present major infection risks, as they have done throughout history. Aeroplanes landing in malarial zones are fumigated with insecticide before leaving to ensure that mosquitoes are not among the passengers, but malaria has spread by this route within Africa and Asia. Global warming may enable it to return to Europe where malaria was once endemic.

The global transport of animals as livestock and as rare species has been similarly important in disseminating certain human infectious diseases, particularly West Nile fever; a possible source of the outbreak in New York in 1999 was exotic birds imported by the city zoo. The smuggling into Europe of infected 'bush meat' from Africa and the Caribbean is another route by which zoonoses can reach new continents. Infected meat in untreated catering 'swill' is the most likely source of the UK epidemic of foot and mouth disease in 2001. Raw foods are increasingly transported from tropical locations to markets where they are 'out of season', bringing infection with them; for example, a major outbreak of gastrointestinal infection in the USA in 1996–1997 was traced to a shipment of raspberries imported from South America.

⬭ What factors other than global trade and transport, population migration and tourism, may have contributed to the emerging infectious disease patterns outlined in Points 1–3, listed in Section 1.4.1 (see p. 22)?

⬬ Concerns have been expressed that global climate change is altering the distribution of vector-borne diseases, for example by extending the geographical range of mosquitoes and other insect vectors. Droughts and flooding have increased in some areas, spreading disease as people are displaced from their lands. Agriculture and exploitation of tropical rainforests (e.g. by logging and cattle ranching in South America) have brought humans into contact with 'novel' pathogens for the first time. Irrigation has created new habitats for disease vectors and transmission routes for water-borne infections.

The evidence that climate change is altering disease patterns is open to question and the data are currently weak. However, Figure 1.8 (overleaf) presents one analysis of the impact of extreme weather events on outbreaks of six emerging infectious diseases globally (and respiratory illness due to fire and smoke resulting from bushfires in drought regions) between June 1997 and May 1998. Flooding is thought to lead to an upsurge in malaria and other fevers transmitted by mosquitoes breeding in stagnant pools.

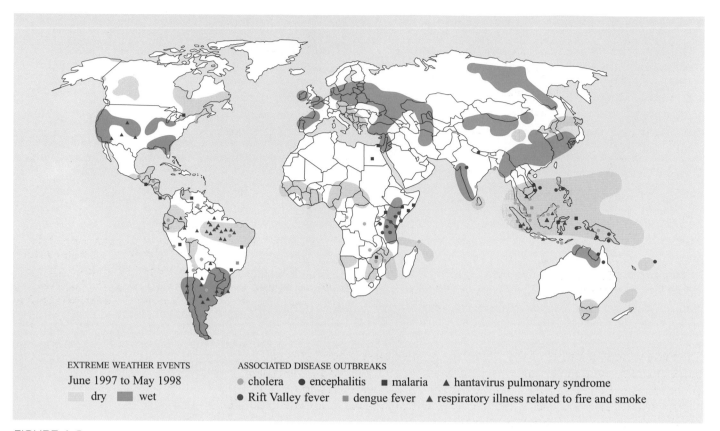

FIGURE 1.8 Associations between extreme wet or dry weather events during 1997–1998, and outbreaks of cholera, encephalitis, malaria, hantavirus pulmonary syndrome, Rift Valley fever, dengue fever, and respiratory illness due to fire and smoke.

Farming practices have also been the direct cause of human infection. The human prion disease vCJD was first identified in the UK in 1996 and is believed to have been transmitted by infected beef from cattle suffering from BSE (bovine spongiform encephalopathy). BSE had spread through the national herd due to the routine practice of rendering down animal offal for incorporation in cattle feed. Intensive farming methods also contributed to the rising UK trend in gastrointestinal diseases (Figure 1.9), including those due to *Salmonella* bacteria in eggs and poultry. Other industries can also be held to blame: cholera bacteria may have been reintroduced to South America in contaminated ballast water discharged into the sea by a ship. (More on cholera is given in the case study associated with Book 2.)

The evolution of more life-threatening strains of food-borne bacteria and the increase in the incidence of these diseases (Points 4 and 5 on page 23) may be partly due to cultural changes in methods of food preparation, including inadequate re-heating of food in domestic microwave ovens and the widespread use of 'cook–chill' processes in industrial kitchens. (More information on controlling food-borne infection in the UK can be found in Book 7.)

The cultural change that has aroused the greatest international concern in the context of emerging infectious diseases relates to medical practice. The appearance of drug-resistant strains of infectious agents (Point 6 on p. 23), particularly **antibiotic-resistant bacteria**, has been driven partly by the indiscriminate prescription of antibiotics by doctors in wealthy countries since the 1970s, and the uncontrolled sale of antibiotics 'over the counter' in poor countries (Box 1.4; the biological mechanisms underlying bacterial resistance are discussed in Book 2).

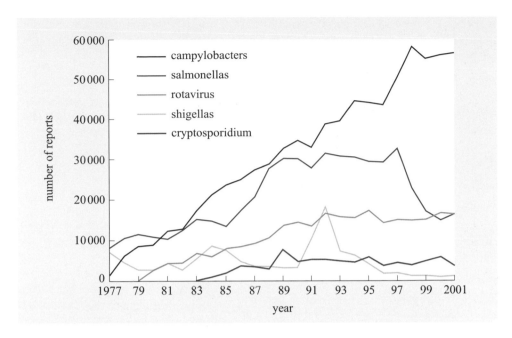

FIGURE 1.9
Trends in selected gastrointestinal pathogens, England and Wales, 1977–2001. The problem of distinguishing rising disease rates from improved detection rates is referred to in Section 1.5.3.

The massive routine use of antibiotics as growth promoters in the livestock industry and the addition of antibacterial chemicals to a wide range of household goods are also thought to have played a part. Drug-resistance has undoubtedly accelerated the TB pandemic (Point 1, above), and contributed to the rise in hospital acquired infections (the subject of Chapter 4).

BOX 1.4   Selection pressure and antibiotic resistance

The bacterial population in an individual human consists of many millions of bacterial cells, varying in their genetic susceptibility to a particular antibiotic. When treated, the most susceptible bacteria die first, so the proportion of more resistant bacteria *increases* in the population over time. The antibiotic is exerting **selection pressure** on individual bacteria, and driving the bacterial population towards greater **antibiotic resistance**. If an optimal dose of the antibiotic is administered for long enough it could kill even the most resistant bacteria. But if these conditions are not met, some of the most resistant variants will survive to re-populate the person and be passed on to others, all of whom now need even stronger doses of that antibiotic to eradicate the infection. If this cycle is repeated often enough, the proportion of antibiotic-resistant bacteria rises so high that the drug becomes useless. A similar process occurs in the evolution of drug-resistant viruses, fungi and parasites.

The impact of political instability has raised the prospect of bioterrorism, although technical difficulties make this an unlikely source of mass infection (Point 8 on p. 23). But conflicts in many parts of the world continue to displace millions of people from their homes into refugee camps where infections flourish, spreading as people disperse. The ideology of certain political regimes has been a major factor in some epidemics, most obviously in South Africa, where the policy of apartheid separated the black male workforce in the country's vast mining industry from their families. TB spread in the crowded conditions in mines and mining hostels, and prostitution flourished; when men returned home they transported HIV to rural areas where TB was already endemic.

These examples draw attention to the fact that poverty and disadvantage, both at the individual and the national level, are among the most important and intractable forces shaping the patterns of infectious disease within and between countries, in advanced economies like the UK and the USA no less than in the developing world.

1.4.3 Infection and degenerative diseases

The 1990s saw a growing body of evidence that infectious agents are contributory factors in at least some **degenerative diseases**, in which tissues and organs gradually 'wear out' or malfunction, generally but not exclusively in later life. These conditions are all **multifactorial disorders**, with complex causation involving the interaction of a number of factors in their onset and progression.

One significant success from using such evidence is shown in Figure 1.10. Preventive treatment with antibiotics has sharply reduced the *incidence* (Box 1.5) of duodenal ulcers. Before about 1993, they were believed to be due to inflammation caused by over-production of digestive acid, and standard treatments aimed to reduce acid secretions in the gut. Then it was discovered that most patients were infected with *Helicobacter*, and that the ulcers could be 'cured' by antibiotics.

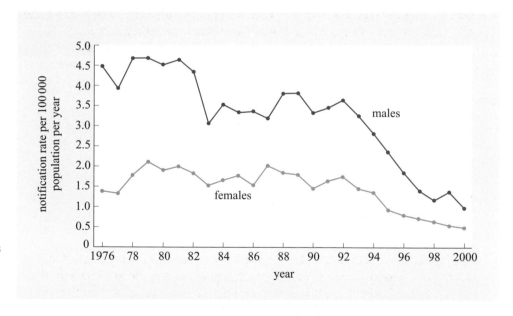

FIGURE 1.10

Mean weekly incidence (number of new cases notified by GPs, per 100 000 population) of duodenal ulcers in males and females (all ages combined), England and Wales, 1976–2000.

Viruses are involved in the aetiology of certain multi-factorial cancers: papilloma virus in cancers of the cervix and penis, hepatitis B and C viruses in liver cancer, and a herpes virus (HHV8) in Kaposi's sarcoma, a common cancer among people infected with HIV. Infection may be a precipitating factor in **autoimmune diseases** (e.g. multiple sclerosis, rheumatoid arthritis), in which the immune system mounts an attack against specific tissues in the patient's own body. More controversial is the possibility that certain neuropsychiatric disorders might also be autoimmune conditions triggered by infections in the brain.

Infection might also possibly play a role in heart disease and strokes by initiating inflammation in blood vessel walls, which in turn promotes the atherosclerotic

> ### BOX 1.5   Incidence and prevalence rates and 'population at risk'
>
> The commonest ways of expressing morbidity data are in terms of **incidence** (new cases arising in a given period, usually a year), and **prevalence** (all cases – new and continuing – at a certain time point, or during a specified period). They are both usually expressed as a *rate*, not a 'raw' number. Common conditions may be expressed as the rate per thousand of the population at risk, whereas the impact of rare conditions may be more apparent if the rate is expressed per million or per 100 000. For many diseases or causes of death the **population at risk** is the whole population, since everyone can be affected. But some conditions can only affect a particular subset (for example, deaths in childbirth can only affect women of childbearing age), so expressing the rate in terms of the population at risk is essential. Maternal mortality is thus usually expressed as the rate per 1000 women aged 15–49 years. The incidence and prevalence of the common 'childhood' infections is generally expressed as the rate per 100 000 children aged under 15, which avoids the impact of these diseases being 'diluted' by the inclusion of older age groups, which are rarely affected.

plaques that eventually impede blood flow. Lastly, unusually small bacteria (termed *nanobacteria*) have been found in the centre of kidney stones, perhaps forming the focus for calcium deposits, much as grit initiates pearl formation in oysters. The causality of many of these associations is unproven, but it is clear that pathogens are involved in a wider spectrum of human illness than just infectious disease.

Summary of Section 1.4

1   Since the 1980s, health organizations have identified 175 emerging infectious diseases (EIDs; new, re-emerging or drug-resistant infections), which have increased greatly in human populations over the past two decades, or which threaten to increase in future.

2   International surveillance of EIDs has intensified; some have been made legally notifiable, and the WHO has set up global rapid response teams to attend new outbreaks.

3   The interaction of cultural and biological factors underlies many EIDs, for example increased air travel and intercontinental tourism, global transport of livestock and foodstuffs, logging and agricultural encroachment into formerly pristine habitats, intensive farming practices, 'fast-food' catering, indiscriminate use of antibiotics as a factor in the evolution of antibiotic-resistant bacteria, and (possibly) climate change.

4   There is growing evidence that infectious agents are involved in the aetiology of at least some multifactorial degenerative diseases, including certain cancers, gastrointestinal ulcers, heart disease and autoimmune disorders.

5   For infectious and all other disorders, the incidence (number of new cases per year) and prevalence (total number of individuals affected at a given time point) are calculated on the basis of the rate in the population at risk (i.e. those individuals capable of being affected by that disorder).

1.5 Global epidemiology of infectious disease

The data presented in this section are derived from the study of infectious disease epidemiology (Box 1.6). In Book 6 you will see some examples of epidemiological data, modelling the spread of an infection through a population, and predicting the effect of vaccination rates on the outcome. Here we present a cross-sectional 'snapshot' in 2000 or nearest available date, but it must be kept in mind that this is merely one moment frozen in a dynamically changing picture.

BOX 1.6   Epidemiology, demography, cross-sectional and longitudinal data

Epidemiology involves the collection and statistical analysis of surveillance data on human deaths, diseases and disabilities, looking for patterns in their distribution in populations that suggest hypotheses about underlying causes. Studies often measure whether a condition is more or less prevalent in population sectors distinguished by certain **demographic variables**: most commonly age, sex, marital status, ethnic group, occupation, educational level, and income band or some other measure of material circumstances, such as 'social class' in the UK. Data may be collected from a single place or region in a relatively short period of time (**cross-sectional data**), and sometimes the results are compared with cross-sectional data from other places collected at around the same time. Or surveillance data may be collected from the same place over a long period, at intervals usually of no more than a few years (**longitudinal data**), to track changes in that location over time. Longitudinal trends from different places may also be compared.

1.5.1 Developing countries

In its annual report published in 2002, the WHO highlighted the major infectious causes of death in people aged 0–44 years in Africa and South East Asia (Figure 1.11). In 2000, more than 36 million people were living with HIV infection worldwide – double the number predicted a decade earlier. There were 5.3 million new infections with HIV that year and 3 million deaths from AIDS, 92% of them in developing countries. Also in 2000, two billion people (one third of the global population) were estimated to be carriers of the TB bacterium, 8.8 million developed active disease and 1.9 million died, 84% of them in developing countries. Co-infection with HIV and TB in developing countries is so widespread that TB is the commonest immediate cause of AIDS deaths.

300 million new cases of malaria occurred in developing countries in 2000, and more than 1 million deaths, over 80% of these fatalities in children under 5 years. The morbidity from malaria is huge, as infected individuals may suffer several acute 'crises' of debilitating illness each year. Drug resistance has evolved in the malarial parasite (*Plasmodium* species) and is spreading rapidly, particularly in South East Asia. A further problem is resistance to insecticides in the mosquito vectors of malaria, and the toxicity to humans and wildlife of the most effective chemical, DDT. You will learn more about malaria in Chapter 3.

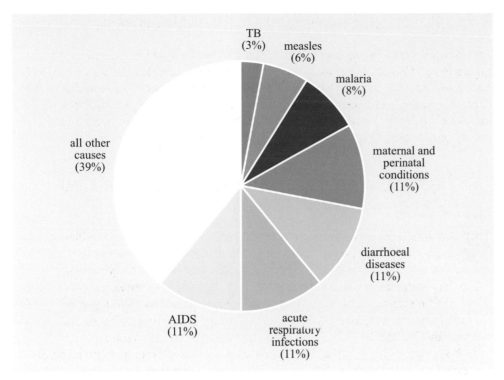

FIGURE 1.11
Proportional mortality due to the most important groups of infectious diseases in African and South East Asian populations aged 0–44 years in 2000. People with AIDS whose immediate cause of death was TB are counted as 'AIDS deaths', a convention that leads to the underestimation of the global impact of TB.

Figure 1.12 shows that in 1999 malaria was ranked fourth in the infectious causes of death among children aged under 5 years in developing countries, after acute respiratory infections (ARIs killed just under 2 million young children in these countries in that year), diarrhoeal diseases (1.7 million) and measles (0.9 million), with AIDS in fifth place (450 000 deaths in the under-fives). Figure 1.12 also shows that ARIs cause more deaths in developing countries than any other category of infectious disease if all ages are combined, and Figure 1.13 (overleaf) reveals the importance of ARIs among young children worldwide.

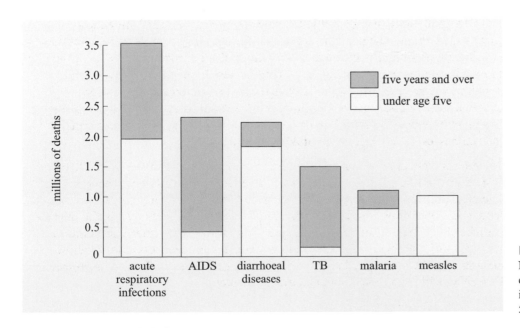

FIGURE 1.12
Numbers of deaths in developing countries in the six leading groups of infectious causes, in people aged under 5 years, or 5 years and over, in 1999.

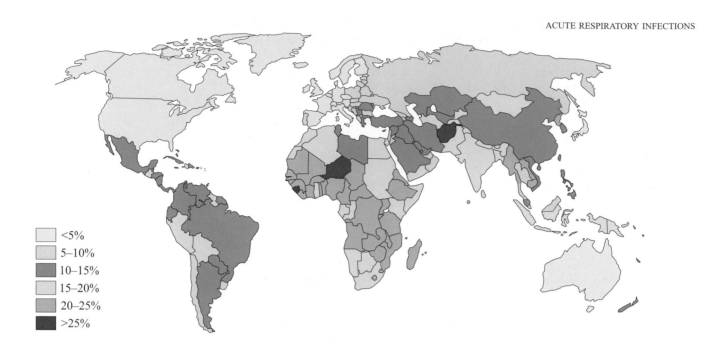

	<5%
	5–10%
	10–15%
	15–20%
	20–25%
	>25%

FIGURE 1.13 Estimates of the percentage of deaths in children aged under 5 years that were attributable to acute respiratory infections (ARIs), by country in 2000. Between 1.6 and 2.2 million young children die each year from ARIs.

From the perspective of a Western industrial economy the catalogue of infectious diseases and their impact on populations in developing countries is unimaginable. In the year 2000, there were 74 laboratory-confirmed cases of measles in England and Wales and 1 death, yet this disease killed almost a million children annually in Africa, Asia and Latin America throughout the 1990s (Figure 1.14). Other infectious diseases that occur all around the world have much higher rates in poor countries than in rich ones: relatively few deaths occur from diarrhoeal diseases in the developed world, but outside these privileged countries they kill over 2 million children and adults every year. Bacterial meningitis has a similar divergence, causing more than 135 000 deaths in developing countries among 1.2 million cases; for comparison, there are around 200 meningitis deaths annually in England and Wales. Over 90% of children in developing countries are believed to be infected with intestinal worms. Over 350 million people globally are chronically infected with hepatitis B virus, primarily in developing countries, resulting in several hundred thousand cases of chronic liver disease and liver cancers annually. The majority of the 340 million new cases of four sexually transmitted infections (syphilis, gonorrhoea, chlamydia and trichomoniasis) that occur each year are also in the developing world.

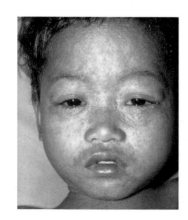

FIGURE 1.14
The face of a child with measles. Children in developing countries who are not vaccinated against the measles virus often develop serious complications, leading to death; malnutrition and other concurrent infections exacerbate the effect of measles on a child, but its scarcity in richer nations disguises the fact that it remains a potentially fatal infection.

Diseases that have not (or not yet) reached the UK persistently ravage populations in poorer countries every year. They include rabies – 30 000 new cases annually in India and 2000 in Bangladesh; yellow fever – 200 000 cases in the tropical regions of Africa and South America; Chagas disease – over one million reported cases; cholera – almost 400 000 cases annually and 11 000 deaths; and African trypanosomes, which cause sleeping sickness in up to half a million people and around 20 000 deaths. One success has been the marked reduction in guinea worm disease, and another is the eradication of polio from many regions of the developing world (both are described in Book 7). However, it is worth placing the current *prevalence* (Box 1.5 on p. 29) of infections in developing countries in context by making three concluding points.

First, with the exception of HIV, TB and sleeping sickness, the underlying trend in most infectious diseases in developing countries has been *downwards* from the mid-nineteenth century onwards, just as in Western Europe and the USA. The conditions that promote infection are being alleviated around the world, and most people in today's devcloping countries experience a lower risk of infection than was the case in pre-industrial Europe.

Second, the decline in infectious diseases has occurred much more slowly outside the wealthy industrialized nations. Infant mortality, which is predominantly due to infectious causes, illustrates this trend. In 1950 the average infant mortality rate for all developing countries combined was 180 per 1000 live births, compared with 56 per 1000 for the developed world. By the year 2000, it had fallen to an average of 65 per 1000 for the developing-country group (i.e. to roughly one third of the rate in 1950), but averaged only 6 per 1000 in developed countries (roughly one tenth of the level in 1950).

Finally, non-infectious causes of death and disability are increasing rapidly in developing countries, particularly the degenerative diseases such as cancers, heart disease and strokes, but also traffic accidents and violence. Thus, the *relative* importance of infectious diseases to human health is declining worldwide. But there are specific exceptions, as Section 1.4 made plain.

1.5.2 Infectious disease in the UK

Against the colossal rates of morbidity and mortality just described for developing countries, it is hard to re-focus and identify infectious diseases as an important threat to health in a country like the UK. However, they contribute a significant proportion of the total burden of illness. Each year 70 000 people die from an infectious disease in England alone (about 15% of all deaths), of which acute respiratory infections (ARI) are the leading cause, as elsewhere in the world. Deaths from infection are predominantly in older age groups, the opposite of the age distribution seen in developing countries now and in developed countries just a century ago (recall Table 1.2). The greatest declines have been in the incidence of vaccine-preventable diseases: the last recorded death from diphtheria in the UK was in 1994; there was one death from measles in the year 2000 and none from whooping cough (pertussis), mumps or rubella; smallpox and polio have been eradicated altogether, and bacterial meningitis and influenza reached an all-time low.

Prevention strategies in the UK are aimed particularly at halting the rise in TB, HIV and other sexually transmitted infections, and food-borne diseases; they must also restore confidence in childhood vaccination programmes after fears were raised in the media about their safety. Health care is now focused primarily on relieving the *morbidity* associated with infection, rather than on preventing deaths.

The most reliable morbidity data come from the weekly returns service from a sample of general practitioners (GPs), who between them report on reasons given for consulting the family doctor in a population of around half a million people in England and Wales. (Figure 1.10, earlier, is based on longitudinal data from this survey; see also Box 1.5.) The numbers of *episodes* of an infectious disease in 2000 as notified by GPs in the sample are given in Table 1.4. Duodenal and gastric ulcers are not included, despite the recently recognized contribution of bacterial infection.

Table 1.4 shows that there were over a quarter of a million notifications by GPs of infectious disease episodes in one year in this sample population of half a million people, which equates to 29 million episodes annually in the UK. However this burden of infectious disease is not evenly distributed: some individuals will consult for an infection several times in a year, and may experience more than one category of infectious disease. The range of infectious and parasitic diseases represented in Table 1.4 is a reminder of their ubiquity: it is rare to get through a year of life without experiencing at least one infection and they are a significant cause of discomfort and debility, lost productivity and missed schooling.

1.5.3 Interpreting epidemiological data

We conclude this chapter by pointing to some reasons for caution in the interpretation of epidemiological data, using examples presented in earlier sections. These points are of general relevance and should be kept in mind as you study the rest of the course.

Sources of uncertainty

The first consideration is whether the data are *complete* and *accurate*. Incomplete surveillance data from countries with poorly funded collection systems are a major problem, and tend to result in underestimates of the burden of infectious disease. Even where the data appear to have come from a reliable source, it is worth considering if they are really as complete as they seem. Table 1.4 can be taken as a pretty good indication of the most prominent infectious causes of morbidity in the UK population as a whole, because it was based on weekly records from such a large population sample. However, it omits two sources of data.

○ Can you say what they are?

● Many episodes of infectious illness are self-treated and are therefore not included in GPs' reports; the cases brought to GPs are only the tip of the 'clinical iceberg'. Also, very severe infections (e.g. bacterial meningitis) may bypass the family doctor altogether and be taken straight to a hospital.

Another common source of uncertainty arises paradoxically from *improvements* in detection methods. An infectious disease may be stable in a population but appear to be increasing over time simply because more cases are being brought to light by increased levels of testing or by new diagnostic tests. For example, the rising trend in *Campylobacter* infections in Figure 1.9 is probably not as acute as it appears; some cases are likely to be due to the rising trend in *testing* for this bacterium.

TABLE 1.4 Number of episodes of infectious and parasitic disease as reported by family doctors sending weekly returns to the Royal College of General Practitioners in 2000, from a sample population of around 500 000 (all ages and both sexes combined) in England and Wales.

Infectious disease	Reported episodes
respiratory infections	
acute bronchitis	35 115
common cold	36 068
influenza/flu-like illnesses	6759
pneumonia/pneumonitis/pleurisy	1273
TB	34
throat infections	32 517
skin infections	22 782
acute ear infections	22 497
urinary tract infections	18 358
intestinal/ diarrhoeal infections	10 713
fungal infections	
candidiasis (thrush)	10 025
ringworm	7991
acute sinusitis	9664
herpes virus infections	
herpes zoster (shingles)	2126
herpes simplex (cold sores)	1836
'childhood infections'	
chickenpox	2382
measles	16
molluscum contagiosum	1497
mumps	80
rubella	22
scarlet fever	428
whooping cough	27
parasitic diseases	
scabies	2696
threadworms	835
Trichomonas vaginalis	45
glandular fever	251
meningitis/encephalitis	80
infective hepatitis	52
all other infectious diseases	38 478
Total	264 601

Conversely, diagnostic *inaccuracy* may inflate the apparent number of cases, particularly where different diseases have signs and symptoms that are difficult to distinguish on the basis of a clinical examination. Accurate diagnosis may require laboratory analysis of samples taken from the patient to identify the causative agent. (Diagnostic methods are discussed in Book 4 of this course.) So for some infectious diseases the number of *clinical diagnoses* can greatly exceed the number of *laboratory-confirmed diagnoses*. For example, in the year 2000, a total of 2378 presumed cases of measles were notified to the disease registry by all the GPs in England and Wales, but only 74 cases were subsequently found to involve measles virus infection.

Allowing for population size

The second point relates to the desirability of using *rates* of morbidity or mortality in the population at risk wherever possible (as in Figures 1.4, 1.5 and 1.10), rather than *numbers* of cases (as in Tables 1.2 and 1.4; Figures 1.6, 1.9 and 1.12). It is particularly important to use rates (not numbers) if you need to compare data from countries or regions with different population sizes. For example, suppose that in a recent year there were 1000 new cases of a certain infectious disease in the USA and 500 new cases in the UK.

○ In which country is it the more serious health problem?

● The current population of the USA (276 million) is over 4.5 times the size of the UK population (58 million), but it has only twice the number of cases of the disease in question. So the infectious disease in this example has a much higher *incidence rate* per million population in the UK than it does in the USA.

A similar problem would arise if you used numbers of cases from the same country over an extended period of time, during which the *size* of the population changed significantly. For example, in 1900 the population of the USA was only 76 million.

○ Explain why Figure 1.4 had to be drawn on the basis of the *rate* of infectious disease mortality, rather than on the annual number of deaths.

● The US population grew from 76 to 276 million over the century depicted. The trend in infectious disease mortality would be grossly distorted if this was ignored. For example, suppose one thousand people died from a certain infection in every year between 1900 and 2000 – the rate of this infection in the population would have declined by almost four-fold, but you would be unable to tell this from the crude number of deaths, which did not change.

The proportional mortality can be expressed on the basis of numbers of deaths (as in Figures 1.3 and 1.11), or on rates in the population at risk, with exactly the same caveats as expressed above. An additional factor to bear in mind when you encounter rates in graphs elsewhere (including in later parts of this course) is that different written conventions can be used to express them. In Figures 1.4, 1.5 and 1.10 we have expressed the population rate as 'per 100 000 per year', but a common alternative form replaces 'per' with a forward slash, as in '/100 000/year'. Scientific notation uses a different convention, replacing 'per' with a superscript (raised) minus one, as in '$100\,000^{-1}\ year^{-1}$'.

Allowing for population age structure

The third point relates to the importance of taking into account differences in population *age structure* when making comparisons between countries, or within the same population over a long period of time. The term 'crude rates' indicates where this has *not* been done (as in Figure 1.4). By contrast, Figure 1.5 uses age-standardized death rates to allow for the fact that the age structure of the population in Britain shifted towards a greater proportion of older and fewer young people between 1860 and 1950, as both birth rates and premature death rates declined. Age standardization is also vital when you are trying to compare data on disease rates between a developed and a developing country, for the following reasons.

In wealthy countries like the UK, a substantial proportion of people live to old age and the birth rate is low, so a relatively small proportion of the population is very young. The reverse is true in poor countries, where the birth rate tends to be very high, so their populations contain a high proportion of children, many of whom die prematurely, leaving relatively few people who survive to old age. Thus, the age structure of populations in developing countries is much 'younger' than in advanced industrial economies. Statistical techniques exist to take account of differences in age structure, which would otherwise have a distorting effect on comparisons, particularly where childhood infections are concerned.

With these points in mind, we hope you can progress with confidence through the epidemiological data presented in the rest of the course.

Summary of Section 1.5

1   Infectious diseases remain the most important cause of death, sickness and disability in developing countries, accounting for around 40% of mortality. However, until the HIV/AIDS pandemic began in the 1980s, the health burden due to infection had been slowly declining to levels below those experienced in pre-industrial Europe.

2   Acute respiratory infections (ARIs) cause the highest levels of mortality of any category of infection worldwide, and among young children they are followed in importance by diarrhoeal diseases, measles and malaria; almost all deaths from malaria occur in developing countries. Many other infections that cause major mortality in developing countries are less often fatal in the developed world (e.g. hepatitis B, bacterial meningitis) or are not present (e.g. cholera, sleeping sickness, yellow fever, plague).

3   The UK illustrates the pattern in Western industrial countries, where infectious diseases now account for around 15% of deaths, mainly in older people. In the UK population of 58 million, an estimated 29 million episodes of infection annually result in a GP consultation. The incidence of vaccine-preventable diseases has declined to very low levels.

4   Caution must be exercised when interpreting epidemiological data, which may be distorted by incomplete surveillance, changes in detection methods and diagnostic inaccuracy. Data based on crude numbers of disease episodes or deaths can be misleading where population size and/or age structure has changed over time or differs between locations; age standardization and the expression of data as a rate in the population at risk improves the reliability of comparisons.

Learning outcomes for Chapter 1

When you have studied this chapter, you should be able to:

1.1   Define and use, or recognise definitions and applications of, each of the terms printed in **bold** in the text. (*Question 1.1*)

1.2   Describe or interpret examples of how the adoption of agriculture and pastoralism, the colonization of other continents by European settlers, and the existence of trade routes and military campaigns, influenced the global distribution of populations and the evolution of infectious diseases. (*Questions 1.2 and 1.4*)

1.3   Compare the main patterns of infectious disease in developed and developing countries in the twentieth century, and illustrate the relative contributions of medical interventions, public health strategies and changes in living standards to the downward trend in mortality and morbidity rates. (*Question 1.3*)

1.4   Taking a global perspective, review a range of possible factors contributing to emerging infectious diseases (EIDs) since the 1980s, and illustrate each factor with examples. (*Question 1.4*)

1.5   Comment on possible sources of inaccuracy in surveillance data and explain why population size, age structure and the population at risk must be taken into account when interpreting epidemiological data on the mortality, morbidity, prevalence and incidence of infectious disease. (*Question 1.5*)

Questions for Chapter 1

Question 1.1

(a) Which of the following infectious diseases are due to zoonoses, according to the WHO definition given in this chapter, and (b) which are transmitted by insect vectors?

- malaria;
- TB;
- sleeping sickness;
- plague.

Question 1.2

In 1817, the East India Company deployed its substantial army against the troops loyal to various local princes and tribal leaders in the region then known as Bengal, in fierce campaigns to acquire territory for commercial exploitation. According to European historians, before that date cholera was endemic in Bengal but occurred only rarely elsewhere in the Indian sub-continent. How did this military action influence the subsequent history of cholera as a force in human history?

Question 1.3

Identify at least one similarity and one significant difference between the infectious disease patterns in developing countries at the end of the twentieth century and those of Western Europe in the pre-industrial period (i.e. before about 1850).

Question 1.4

What consequence for human infectious disease is believed to have followed the adoption of pastoralism around 10 000 years ago, and how might pastoralism still be exerting an influence in the present on certain categories of emerging infectious diseases?

Question 1.5

The population of Scotland has been stable at just over 5 million people since the 1950s and is predicted to remain so for at least the next 20 years. However, the age structure has been shifting towards an older profile and this trend is expected to accelerate in the future. Between 1991 and 2000 there was a fall of 2% in the proportion aged under 14 years, and a further fall of 16% in this age group is projected to occur by 2021.

(a) Why must the change in age structure be taken into account when evaluating trends in childhood infectious diseases in Scotland?

(b) Explain why children are the principal 'population at risk' from infections such as measles.

2 INFLUENZA: A CASE STUDY

We have chosen influenza as the first case study in this course for a number of reasons. To start with, most people have suffered from flu at some time in their lives, so you will probably have personal experience or a good idea of the symptoms and progression of the disease. Secondly, influenza is one of the world's most serious diseases. The pandemic of flu that occurred in 1918, immediately following the First World War, is thought to have killed up to 20 million people, more than died in the war itself. Finally, influenza illustrates many important ideas concerning infectious diseases, which will be taken up at different points later in the course. In the final book of the course we look at different strategies of controlling disease. Influenza is an example of a disease that is controlled most effectively by vaccination, and the information you derive from each of the other subject areas will help you understand why this is so.

2.1 Background and introduction

Influenza as a disease has been recognized for centuries, even though the viruses which cause the disease were not correctly identified until 1933. Indeed the name itself is derived from an Italian word, and reflected the widespread belief, held in medieval times, that the disease was caused by an evil climatic *influence* due to an unfortunate alignment of the stars. Our current understanding, that infectious diseases are caused by infectious agents, is so ingrained that such ideas now seem absurd. However, even during the Middle Ages, people had a sound idea of infection and realized that some diseases could be passed from one individual to another and others could not. For example, the use of quarantine for a disease such as plague, but not for many other illnesses, shows that people could distinguish infectious disease from non-infectious diseases even if the causative agent and the method of transmission were obscure.

The idea that influenza is caused by the influence of the stars was perhaps not a satisfactory explanation of how the disease spread, even in those times. However it does identify an important feature of flu – that serious epidemics of the disease occur at irregular intervals. For example, in the twentieth century there were at least five major epidemics of flu that spread around the world (a pandemic), and there were less serious epidemics in most years. In times when people believed in the spontaneous generation of life, the stars would have seemed a reasonable explanation for some unpleasant and unexpected epidemic. Interestingly, the medieval view of flu epidemics originating in the stars lingered on into the late twentieth century, when it was proposed that flu viruses seeded the earth from asteroids. Now however, we know that the disease is caused by a specific group of viruses that evolve in humans and other animals, and that recovery and immunity are functions of the immune system. Therefore any explanation of the epidemic patterns of flu must be based on virology, immunology and epidemiology.

☐ How would you define 'influenza'?

■ You may well have defined influenza as an infection caused by an influenza virus. However, you may have defined it according to its symptoms: an infection that starts in the upper respiratory tract, with coughing and sneezing, spreads to give aching joints and muscles, and produces a fever that makes you feel awful; but usually it has gone in 5–10 days and people make a full recovery.

The first definition here is the biological definition, and in this course we define diseases according to the infectious agent which produces them. The reason for this is that different infections can produce the same symptoms, and the same infectious agent can produce quite different symptoms in different people, depending on their age, genetic make-up or the tissue of the body that becomes infected. Here we make the distinction between the infectious disease caused by a particular agent and the disease symptoms. Unfortunately there is a lot of confusion in common parlance about different diseases. Often, people will say that they have 'a bit of flu' when they have an infection with some other virus or bacterium that produces flu-like symptoms. Such loose terminology is understandable, since most people are firstly concerned with the symptoms of their disease. But to treat and control disease requires accurate identification of the causative agent, so this will be our starting point for considering any infectious disease.

Consider the description below, written by Thucydides in 430 BC as 'plague' swept through Athens during the Peloponnesian War:

> People who were fit and healthy suddenly felt hot, feverish pains in the head: the eyes became red and inflamed, bleeding took place in the throat and tongue, and the breath was abnormal and fetid. Sneezing and hoarseness followed, and the disease soon moved down to the chest with painful coughing. When it settled in the abdomen, it produced stomach upsets and vomiting of every type of bile known to doctors, with great distress to the sick. Most people suffered from empty retching and strong spasms; for some the retching ended at this stage of the disease, for others much later.

> The surface of the body was not particularly hot to the touch, nor was the patient pale; the skin was somewhat red, blotched and covered with small pustules and ulcers. Internally however the fever was so great that not even the lightest clothing was tolerable and people wanted only to be naked, and most of all to plunge into cold water. Many actually did so, if they were not looked after, flinging themselves into water-tanks because of their unquenchable thirst – although it made no difference whether they drank much or little. Worst of all was the inability to stay still and the lack of sleep.

> As long as the disease was at its height, the body did not waste away but showed unexpected resistance to the pain. Consequently, most died on the sixth or eighth day from internal fever with some strength still left in them; or, if they survived beyond this, mostly died from the weakness caused by the disease affecting the bowels with ulceration and excessive diarrhoea.

The description of the symptoms is very vivid, and it has been argued that this was an ancient epidemic of flu, possibly compounded by bacterial pneumonia and infections of the gut. Nowadays we probably would not equate these symptoms with flu because the description is so remote from our own experience of the disease. However, we should remember that the 1918 flu epidemic killed millions of typically young healthy people within days of infection, so influenza can produce rapid and life-threatening disease. However, other scholars have argued that the epidemic described above was smallpox. The point is made that it really is impossible to say with certainty what disease is described, since we only have the symptoms to go on. Today we identify the disease by the pathogen involved and describe the associated symptoms, which may vary greatly from person to person.

In the section above, the term pathogen was used, meaning an infectious agent which produces damage or disease. How then is a pathogen identified as the causative agent of a particular disease? An important start was made in this area by the German physician Robert Koch, who in 1877 had identified the bacterium that causes anthrax (*Bacillus anthracis*) and demonstrated that it was possible to transmit the disease to mice. He formalized a set of rules for distinguishing a pathogen from a harmless microbe, which just happened to be found in the same patient. These rules came to be called **Koch's postulates**.

1   The organism is regularly found in the lesions of the disease.

2   It can be isolated in pure culture on artificial media.

3   Inoculation of the culture produces a similar disease in experimental animals.

4   The organism can be recovered from lesions in these animals.

Koch's postulates were seen as the 'gold standard' for assigning a pathogen to a disease, but they cannot always be met. For example, some pathogens, including viruses can only live inside cells and therefore will not grow on artificial media. For many viruses it is now possible to circumvent this limitation by propagating the pathogen in live cells grown in tissue culture.

Koch's third postulate sometimes raises another problem: several pathogens infect only humans, so it is not possible to transmit disease to an experimental animal. As it happens, influenza does not fall into this category, and different strains of influenza virus infect many species of mammals and birds. Moreover, as you will see later, the strains sometimes move between host species.

The difficulties encountered in assigning a particular pathogen to a disease are well-illustrated by influenza. During the influenza pandemic that occurred in 1890, the microbiologist Pfeiffer isolated a novel bacterium from the lungs of people who had died of flu. The bacterium was named *Haemophilus influenzae* and since it was the only bacterium that could be regularly cultivated from these individuals at autopsy, it was assumed that *H. influenzae*[1] was the causative agent of flu. Again, in the 1918 flu pandemic, the bacterium could be regularly cultivated from people who had died of flu with pneumonia. So it was thought that flu was caused by the bacterium, and *H. influenzae* came to be called the 'influenza bacillus'. The role of *H. influenzae* was only brought into question in 1933, when Smith, Andrews and Laidlaw showed that it was possible to transfer a flu-like illness from nasal washings of an infected person to ferrets, using a bacteria-free filtrate. These studies paved the way to the identification of influenza viruses (Figure 2.1). A fortunate step in this process was the discovery that the virus could be grown in chick embryos (fertilized eggs), so for influenza it was eventually possible to fulfil Koch's postulates to identify the causative agent.

○   Why do you suppose that *H. influenzae* was incorrectly identified as the causative agent of flu?

[1] The conventions for abbreviating bacterial names are given in Book 2.

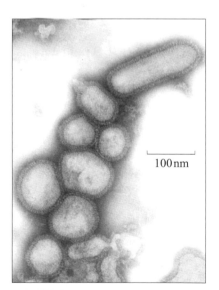

FIGURE 2.1
Influenza virus. Flu viruses are small viruses that use RNA as their genetic material. They have irregular shapes and the outer envelope, derived from the plasma membrane of the host cell, contains viral proteins, which are visible in this electron micrograph.

100nm

■ Since it is regularly found in serious flu infections, and since it can be cultured in pure form on artificial media, it fulfilled two of Koch's postulates. Moreover, at that time no-one knew what a virus was, and everyone was thinking in terms of bacterial causes for infectious diseases.

Although the precise role of *H. influenzae* in the 1890 and 1918 flu pandemics is not clear, it is likely that the bacteria were present and acting in concert with the flu virus to produce the pneumonia. Synergy between virus and bacteria was demonstrated by Shope, who infected pigs with swine influenza virus with or without the bacteria. He showed that the disease produced by the bacteria and virus together was more severe than that produced by either one alone. In its role of copathogen, *H. influenzae* is only one of a number of bacteria that can exacerbate the viral infection. This highlights a very important point. In the tidy world of a microbiology or immunology laboratory scientists typically examine the effect of one infectious agent in producing disease. In the real world, people often become infected with more than one pathogen. Indeed, infection with one agent often lays a person open to infection with another, as immune defences become overwhelmed. For this reason, a particular disease as seen by physicians may be due to a combination of pathogens.

Let us list some important points that the study of flu raises.

1   A single pathogen can produce different types of disease in different people. Genetic variation in a pathogen can also affect the type of disease it produces. *To understand this we need to know something of the genetic and social differences in the host population, and of the diversity of the pathogen.*

2   The symptoms of a particular disease may be produced by different pathogens or by a combination of pathogens. *To understand this requires some knowledge of pathology and cell biology.*

3   Some diseases, such as flu, affect humans and several other animal species, whereas others are more selective in their host range. *The basic biology of different pathogens underlies these differences.*

4   Flu is a disease that can be contracted several times during a lifetime, but many other infectious diseases are only ever contracted once. *To understand this we need to look at how the immune system reacts to different pathogens, and how responses vary depending on the pathogen.*

5   Outbreaks of flu occur regularly, but some epidemics are much more serious than others. *This requires an understanding of aspects of virology, immunology, evolutionary biology and epidemiology.*

Later on we look into all these different areas in some detail, but, to begin, we use influenza as an example to introduce them.

2.1.1 Influenza in humans

Influenza is an acute viral disease that affects the respiratory tract in humans. The virus is spread readily in aerosol droplets produced by coughing and sneezing, which are symptoms of the illness. Other symptoms include fatigue, muscle and joint pains and fever. Following infection, the virus replicates in the cells lining the upper and lower respiratory tract. Virus production peaks 1–2 days later, and virus particles are shed in secretions over the following 3–4 days. During this period, the patient is infectious and the symptoms are typically at their most severe. After one week, virus is no longer produced, although it is possible to detect viral *antigens* (see Box 2.1) for up to two weeks. Immune responses are initiated immediately the virus starts to replicate, and *antibodies* against the virus start to appear in the blood at 3–4 days post infection. These continue to increase over the following days and persist in the blood for many months. In a typical flu infection, the virus is completely eliminated within two weeks. This is sterile immunity, as described in Chapter 1: the virus cannot be recovered from the patient after recovery from the disease. Figure 2.2 shows the typical time course of an acute flu infection.

BOX 2.1   Antigens and antibodies

An **antigen** was originally defined as any molecule which the body recognizes as 'non-self', and against which an **antibody** is produced. Antibodies are glycoproteins that are produced by B lymphocytes, and which bind specifically, but non-covalently, to the inducing antigen. The definition of an antigen has now been extended to include any molecule that the body can recognize as foreign; this includes the fragments of molecules which are recognized by T lymphocytes. In the broadest sense, it has always been known that the immune system can also recognize self molecules, even if it does not usually react against them. Consequently, the widest definition of an antigen is a molecule that can be recognized by the immune system, of which there are conventional non-self antigens and self molecules or autoantigens.

Antibodies are also known as immunoglobulins (Ig), because they are globular proteins involved in immunity. They come in five classes, each of which is structurally different and has different functions. The classes are IgG, IgA, IgM, IgD and IgE; these are explained in more detail in Book 3.

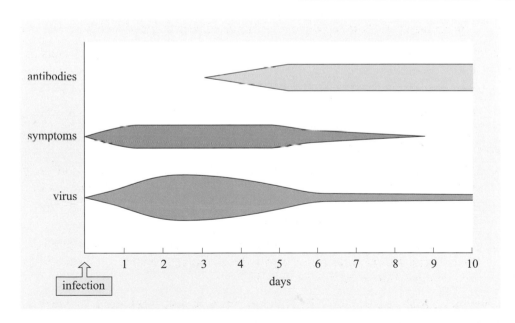

FIGURE 2.2
Time course of a typical flu infection. Production of the virus starts early after infection and is maximal within two days. The infection is contained during this period by various immune defences. Specific antibody production starts to appear by day 3, and this contributes to the elimination of the virus. Symptoms coincide with the production of the virus.

For infants, older people, and those with other underlying diseases (e.g. of the heart or respiratory system) an infection with flu may prove fatal. However, the severity of a flu epidemic and case fatality rate depends on the **strain** of flu involved (see Box 2.2 on p. 47) and the level of immunity in the host population. During a severe epidemic, there are typically thousands more deaths in the UK than would normally be expected for that time of year, and these can be attributed to the disease. Although older people are usually most at risk from fatal disease, this is not always so. In the 1918 flu pandemic there was a surprisingly high death rate in people aged 20–40 (Figure 2.3 overleaf).

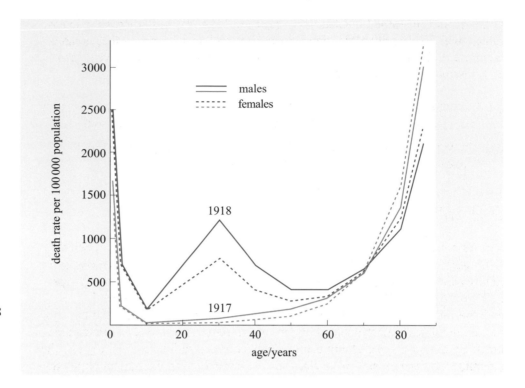

FIGURE 2.3
Mortality according to age in the 1918 US flu epidemic, 1917 and 1918 rates in males and females. This epidemic was notable because it particularly affected people aged 20–40 years.

○ Why do you suppose that older people are usually more at risk from infectious disease than younger people? In what circumstances might older people be more resistant to infection than young people?

● Older people may have a less effective immune response, or a reduced capacity for repair and regeneration of tissues. However, if they have previously encountered a disease (in their youth) they could retain some immunity and be less susceptible than younger people who have not contracted the disease before.

2.1.2 Influenza infection in other species

Influenza viruses infect a wide range of species, including pigs, horses, ducks, chickens and seals. In most of these other species the virus produces an acute infection. For example, in most of the mammals the symptoms are very similar to those in humans: an acute infection of the respiratory tract, which is controlled by the immune response although fatal infections occur in some species. However, in wild ducks and other aquatic birds the virus primarily infects the gut and the birds do not appear to have any physical symptoms. Despite this, ducks may remain infected for 2–4 weeks and during this time they shed virus in their faeces. Potentially this is a very important reservoir of infection; although flu viruses do not often cross the species barrier, the pool of viruses present in other species is an important genetic reservoir for the generation of new flu viruses that do infect humans.

When we consider strategies for controlling a disease, the presence of an animal reservoir of infection is very important. For example, an immunization programme against flu would substantially reduce the incidence of the disease in humans, but is unlikely to eradicate it, since there is always a reservoir of these viruses in other animals. As you learned in Chapter 1, it is useful to distinguish diseases such as rabies, which primarily affect other vertebrates and occasionally infect humans (zoonoses), from diseases such as flu where different strains of the virus can affect humans or other animals.

○ Can you identify any fundamental difference between the way that zoonoses (e.g. rabies) are transmitted, and the way in which flu is transmitted?

● Flu can be transmitted from one human being to another, whereas most zoonoses, including rabies, are not transmitted between people.

2.2 Influenza viruses

Viruses are classified into different families, groups and subgroups in much the same way as are species of animals or plants. The influenza viruses belong to a family called the Orthomyxoviruses (see Box 2.2), which fall into three groups: influenza A, B and C. Type A viruses are able to infect a wide variety of endothermic (warm-blooded) animals, including mammals and birds, and analysis of their genomes indicates that all strains of influenza-A originated from aquatic birds. By contrast, types B and C are mostly confined to humans. At any one time, a number of different strains of virus may be circulating in the human population.

BOX 2.2   Families, groups and strains of virus and the role of serology

Viruses were originally classified into different groups according to similarities in their structure, mode of replication and disease symptoms. For example the Orthomyxoviruses include viruses that cause different types of influenza, while Paramyxoviruses include the viruses that cause measles and mumps. Such large groupings are often called a *family* of viruses. The families can be subdivided into smaller groups, such as influenza A, B and C. Even within a single such group of viruses there can be an enormous level of genetic diversity, and this is the basis of the different strains. As an example, two HIV particles from the same individual may be 4% different in their genome; compare this with the 1% difference between the genomes of humans and chimpanzees, which are different species. At one time, strain differences were determined by the ability of different antibodies to distinguish them (serology), but with advances in molecular biology a strain is now usually defined by its genetic makeup, although serology is still useful. Because of their genetic diversity, a viral strain can encompass a considerable amount of genetic variation.

The **genome** of an organism is the complete set of genes that it contains. The genome of flu viruses consists of negative-sense single-stranded RNA (Box 2.3). The total genome is segmented, meaning that there are seven or eight fragments of RNA encoding approximately 14 proteins. Understanding the way in which different viruses replicate is important, since it allows the identification of particular points in their life-cycle that may be susceptible to treatment with antiviral drugs.

Box 2.3   **Viral genomes**

Viruses have very diverse genomes. Whereas the genomes of bacteria, plants and animals are of DNA, genomes of viruses can be constituted from either DNA or RNA. Usually, DNA is a double-stranded molecule with paired, complementary strands (dsDNA) and RNA is a single stranded molecule (ssRNA). However, some viruses have single-stranded DNA genomes (ssDNA) and some have double-stranded RNA genomes (dsRNA). The type of nucleic acid found in the genome depends on the group of viruses involved.

RNA encodes protein in all living creatures, and the sequence of bases in the RNA determines the sequence of amino acids in the protein. A strand of RNA which has the potential to encode protein is said to be 'positive sense'. If a strand of RNA is complementary to this, then it is 'negative sense'. Negative-sense RNA or DNA must first be copied to a complementary positive-sense strand of RNA before it can be translated into protein. The description of the influenza genome as negative-sense ssRNA means that its RNA cannot be translated without copying first.

The structure of influenza-A is shown schematically in Figure 2.4. The viral RNA is enclosed by nucleoproteins to make a ribonucleoprotein complex (RNP), and this is contained in the central core of the virus, called the **capsid**. The nucleoproteins are required for viral replication and packing of the genome into the new capsid, which is formed by M-protein (or matrix protein). The M-protein is the most abundant component of the virus, constituting about 40% of the viral mass; it is essential for the structural integrity of the virus and to control assembly of the virus.

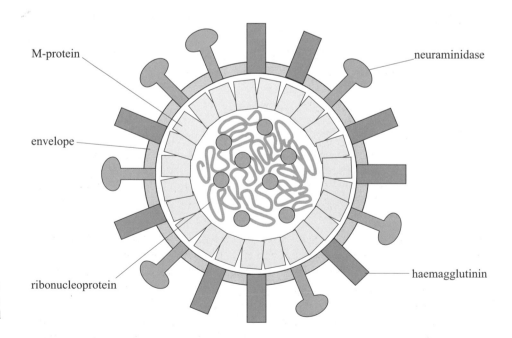

FIGURE 2.4
Structure of an influenza-A virus. The viral core or capsid, formed by M-protein, also contains the viral genome and a number of enzymes required for viral replication. The genome of the virus consists of eight separate strands of RNA, which are associated with nucleoproteins. The viral envelope is a lipid bilayer formed from the plasma membrane of the host cell, which contains two virus-encoded proteins, haemagglutinin and neuraminidase.

Orthomyxoviruses are a group of viruses in which the capsid is surrounded by a phospholipid bilayer derived from the plasma membrane of the cell that produced the virus, as shown in Figure 2.4, called the **viral envelope**. Two proteins, haemagglutinin and neuraminidase, are expressed on the envelope. These proteins are encoded by the virus and are inserted into the plasma membrane of the infected cell before the newly-produced virus buds off from the cell surface.

The haemagglutinin can bind to glycophorin, a type of polysaccharide that contains sialic acid residues, and which is present on the surface of a variety of host cells. The virus uses the haemagglutinin to attach to the cells that it will infect. Antibodies against haemagglutinin are therefore particularly important in limiting the spread of the virus, since they prevent it from attaching to new host cells.

Neuraminidase is an enzyme that cleaves sialic acid residues from polysaccharides. It has a role in clearing a path to the surface of the target cell before infection, and it promotes release of the budding virus from the cell surface after infection.

The structures of influenza-B and influenza-C are broadly similar to that of Type A, although in influenza-C the functions of the haemagglutinin and the neuraminidase are combined in a single molecule, haemagglutinin esterase. Influenza-C does not normally cause clinical disease or epidemics, so the following discussion is confined to influenza-A and B.

2.2.1 Designation of strains of influenza

A considerable number of genetically different strains of influenza-A have been identified, and these are classified according to where they were first isolated and according to the type of haemagglutinin and neuraminidase they express. For example A/Shangdong/9/93(H3N2) is an influenza-A virus isolated in Shangdong in 1993 – the 9th isolate in that year – and it has haemagglutinin type 3 and neuraminidase type 2. At least 15 major variants of haemagglutinin have been recognized, but to date most of these have only been found in birds.

The designation for influenza-B is similar, but omits the information on the surface molecules, for example B/Panama/45/90.

As you will see later, accurate identification of different strains of flu is crucial if we are to control epidemics by vaccination programmes.

2.2.2 Infection and replication

If you are unfamiliar with the basic biology of viruses, you may prefer to skip this section now and return to it after you have accessed the relevant material from S204 Book 4 that we have provided on the Reference CD-ROM, and also studied Book 2 (*Infectious Agents*) in this course. If you have already studied a Level 2 biology course (e.g. S204), read on.

The replication cycle of influenza is illustrated in Figure 2.5 overleaf. Influenza is spread in aerosol droplets that contain virus particles, and infection may occur if these come into contact with the epithelium in the respiratory tract. At this stage the neuraminidase is able to cleave polysaccharides in mucus coating the tract, which allows the virus to reach the surface of the respiratory epithelium. The haemagglutinin now attaches to glycophorins on the surface of the host cell, and the virus is taken up by endocytosis into a phagosome. Lysosomes fuse with the

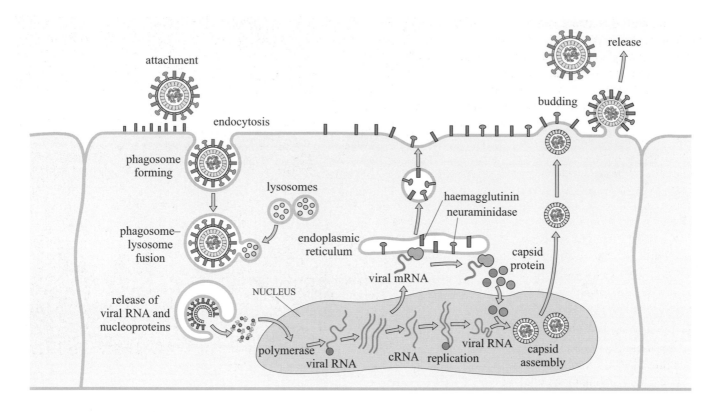

FIGURE 2.5 Replication cycle of a flu virus. The virus attaches to glycophorins on the surface of a cell via its haemagglutinin. After endocytosis into a phagosome and acidification of the phagosome by lysosomes, the virus fuses with the phagosomal membrane, releasing its genomic RNA into the cytosol. The viral RNA migrates to the nucleus and is replicated by polymerases to produce viral complementary RNA (cRNA), which is replicated again to produce new viral genomic RNA. Viral messenger RNA (mRNA) is used to translate the haemagglutinin and neuraminidase on the endoplasmic reticulum, and these proteins are transported to the cell membrane. Other proteins are translated in the cytoplasm and used for assembly of viral capsids in the nucleus. The capsids bud off from the cell surface, taking a segment of cell membrane containing the haemagglutinin and neuraminidase, and this forms the new viral envelope.

phagosome to form a phagolysosome and the pH inside the phagolysosome falls. This promotes fusion of the viral envelope with the membrane of the phagolysosome, causing the viral capsid to release the viral RNA and nucleoproteins into the cytosol of the cell.

After release into the cytosol, the viral genomic RNA migrates to the nucleus where transcription of viral mRNA and replication of the viral genome occurs. These processes require both host and viral enzymes. The viral negative-stranded RNA is replicated by an RNA-dependent RNA polymerase, producing a double-stranded RNA intermediate. The positive-sense RNA so generated acts as mRNA for translation of viral proteins. Production of the viral proteins takes place on the host cell's ribosomes, in the cytosol and on the endoplasmic reticulum. The infection cycle is rapid and viral molecules can be detected within the host cell within an hour of the initial infection.

Production of the viral genomic RNA is activated by viral proteins and is carried out by the same RNA polymerase as initiated the primary replication. The viral genome is produced from a complementary strand of RNA (cRNA) which is positive stranded, but is structurally slightly different to the viral mRNA. Replication of the positive sense cRNA produces the negative-stranded genomic RNA required for new viral particles.

The viral capsid is also assembled within the nucleus of the infected cell, while the envelope glycoproteins (haemagglutinin and neuraminidase) are translated in the endoplasmic reticulum, processed and transported to the cell's plasma membrane. The capsid moves to the plasma membrane, where it buds off, taking a segment of membrane with it to form the new viral envelope. Influenza virus budding from the surface of an infected cell is shown in Figure 2.6.

○ From the description above, can you identify a process or element in the replication cycle which is characteristic of the virus, and which would not normally occur in a mammalian cell?

■ The replication of RNA on an RNA template with the production of double-stranded RNA would never normally occur in a mammalian cell. Double stranded RNA is therefore a signature of a viral infection. Significantly, cells have a way of detecting the presence of dsRNA, and this activates a mechanism that limits viral replication. This will be explained further in Book 3 (*Immunology*) when we look at the actions of 'interferons'.

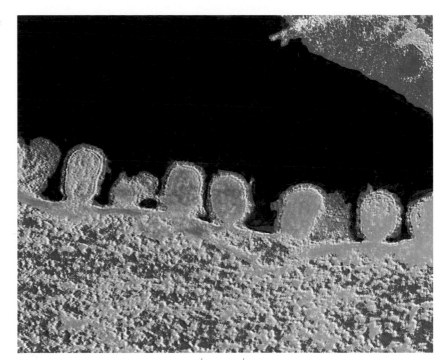

100 nm

FIGURE 2.6
Flu virus particles budding from the surface of an infected cell.

2.2.3 Cellular pathology of influenza infection

Flu viruses can infect a number of different cell types from different species. The cellular glycoproteins which are recognized by viral haemagglutinin are widely distributed, and this partly explains why flu viruses can infect several different cell types in different species. Viruses generally can only replicate in particular types of cell and this property is called their **tropism**. Hence we can say that flu viruses have a broad tropism. A second consideration is that the replication strategy of flu is relatively simple: 'infect the cell, replicate as quickly as possible and then get out again'. The production of large numbers of virus particles will usually kill the infected cell and this is referred to as the **cytopathic effect** of the virus. Cell death caused directly by the virus can be distinguished from cell death caused by the actions of the immune system as it eliminates infected cells.

Cell death impairs the function of an infected organ and induces inflammation, a process that brings white cells (leukocytes) and molecules of the immune system to the site of infection. In the first instance, the leukocytes are involved in limiting the spread of infection; later they become involved in combating the infection, and in the final phase they clear cellular debris so that the tissue can repair or regenerate. The symptoms of flu experienced by an infected person are partly due to the cytopathic effect of the virus, partly due to inflammation and partly a result of the specific immune response against the virus. The severity of the disease largely depends on the rate at which these processes occur. In most instances, the immune response develops sufficiently quickly to control the infection and patients recover.

If viral replication and damage outstrip the development of the immune response then a fatal infection can occur.

In severe infections with flu, the lungs may fill with fluid as the epithelium lining the alveoli (air sacs) are damaged by the virus. The fluid is ideal for the growth of bacteria, and this can lead to a bacterial pneumonia, in which the lungs become infected with one or more types of bacteria such as *Haemophilus influenzae*. Damage to cells lining blood vessels can cause local bleeding into the tissues, and this form of 'fulminating disease' was regularly seen in post-mortem lung tissues of people who died in the 1918 pandemic.

2.3 Patterns of disease

In humans, pigs and horses flu viruses circulate through populations at regular intervals. The disease is endemic in tropical regions (i.e. it is continually present in the community, see Chapter 1). In temperate latitudes, infections are usually seasonal or epidemic, with the greatest numbers occurring in the winter months (Figure 2.7). Epidemics also occur sporadically in sea mammals and poultry, and in these species high mortality is typical. In most years flu in humans affects a minority of the population, the disease course is not very severe and the level of mortality is not great. In such years the influenza virus is slightly different from the previous year due to the accumulation of a number of genetic mutations, a process called **antigenic drift**, through which the molecules present on the surface of the virus change progressively. This means that the immune response which was effective at recognizing and eliminating the virus from the previous year is less effective against the strain from the current year.

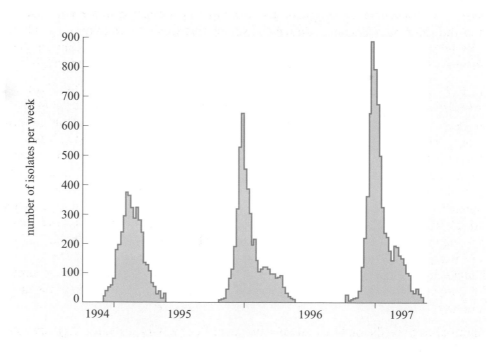

FIGURE 2.7 Epidemic patterns of flu in temperate latitudes. The graph shows notifications of flu in the USA each week from 1994–1997.

At irregular intervals the virus undergoes a major genetic change called an **antigenic shift**. This process only occurs in influenza-A viruses, typically every 10–30 years, and it is associated with severe pandemics, serious disease and high mortality. The pandemics are often named according to the area in the world where they were thought to originate. Evidence suggests, however, that in the twentieth century they all originated in China, with the exception of the 1918 pandemic, which first occurred in the USA. More accurately, the pandemic strains are designated according to their surface antigens – the haemagglutinin (H) and the neuraminidase (N) – that occur in a number of major variants (H0, H1, H2, etc., and N1, N2). The major pandemic strains are described according to which of the variants they possess (Table 2.1).

TABLE 2.1 Major flu pandemic strains.

Year	Designation	Common name
1900	H3N8	–
1918	H1N1	Spanish flu
1957	H2N2	Asian flu
1968	H3N2	Hong Kong flu
1977	H1N1	Russian flu

Since the discovery of the virus in the 1930s it has been possible to isolate and accurately identify each of the epidemic strains, but, as earlier strains of virus have now died out, it has been necessary to infer their identity by examining the antibodies in the serum of affected people. Antibodies and the ability of the immune system to respond to a strain of flu are much more persistent than the virus itself. It is thus possible to analyse antibodies to determine which types of haemagglutinin and neuraminidase they recognize long after the virus itself has gone. One can then deduce which type of influenza virus that person contracted earlier in their life.

In 1997 a new strain of influenza-A, H5N1, was identified in Hong Kong. The strain was rife in chickens and a small number of people had become infected. Mortality in these individuals was very high, (6 of 18 died), and so there was serious concern that it marked the beginning of a new pandemic. The authorities in Hong Kong responded by a mass cull of poultry in the region. No further cases were reported in people and the spread of infection from poultry to humans appeared to have been prevented. Whether the H5N1 outbreak was an isolated incident of a strain spreading from chicken to humans, or whether it was the start of a major pandemic which was nipped in the bud, cannot be known. Subsequent analysis showed that the high virulence of the new strain could partly be related to the new variant of haemagglutinin (H5), and partly to a different type of viral polymerase. This outbreak clearly demonstrates the way in which bird influenza can act as a source of new viral strains, and shows that such new strains may be very dangerous to humans.

In order to track the outbreak of new strains of flu, the World Health Organization (WHO) supports a global surveillance programme. You can visit their FluNet website (see the course website Resources). The WHO has links with sentinel laboratories distributed in different countries throughout the world, which receive and analyse isolates of flu from different regions. The strains are identified, and the information is used to assess potential new pandemics, so that vaccine manufacturers can be alerted and appropriate public health measures taken. The information is also used to identify which strains of flu are prevalent at any one time and the data are used by WHO scientists to help predict which strains should be used in the vaccine preparation for the following year. Typically a flu vaccine contains material from the main influenza-A strains and an influenza-B strain, so that an immune response is induced against the most likely infections. Usually the scientists predict correctly and immunized people are effectively protected against the current strains (>90% protection). However, the prediction is occasionally incorrect, or a new strain develops during the time that the vaccine is being manufactured. In this case the vaccine generally provides poor protection.

◯ What can you deduce about immunity against flu infection from the observations on vaccination above?

◼ The immune response is strain-specific. If you are immunized against the wrong strain of flu, then the response is much less effective and you are more likely to contract the disease.

2.3.1 Immune responses to influenza

The immune system uses different types of immune defence against different types of pathogen – the responses against flu are typical of those which are mounted against an acute viral infection, but different to the responses against infection by bacteria, worms, fungi or protoctist parasites.

When confronted with an acute virus infection, the immune system has two major challenges:

1 The virus replicates very rapidly, killing the cells it infects. Since a specific immune response takes several days to develop, the body must limit the spread of the virus until the immune defences can come into play.

2 Viruses replicate inside cells of the body, but they spread through the host's body in the blood and tissue fluids. Therefore the immune defences must recognize infected cells (intracellular virus) and destroy them. But the immune system must also recognize and eradicate free virus in the tissue fluids (extracellular virus) in order to prevent the virus from infecting new cells.

We briefly consider the kinds of immune defence that the body deploys against flu (Figure 2.8), but a detailed explanation of these defences must wait until the immunology section of the course in Book 3.

How does the body act quickly to limit viral spread? When a virus infects a cell of the body, the molecular machinery for protein synthesis within the cell is usurped as the virus starts to produce its own nucleic acids and proteins. The cell detects the infection and releases signalling molecules called **interferons**, which bind to receptors on neighbouring cells and cause them to synthesize antiviral proteins. If a virus infects such cells they resist viral replication, so fewer viruses are produced and viral spread is delayed.

Also, in the earliest stages of a virus infection the molecules on the cell surface change. Cells lose molecules that identify them as normal 'self' cells. At the same

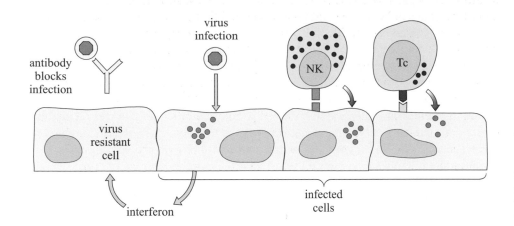

FIGURE 2.8
Immune defences against flu viruses. Antibodies can block the spread of the virus by preventing them from attaching to host cells. Infected cells release interferon, which signals to neighbouring cells to induce resistance. Natural killer cells (NK) and cytotoxic T cells (Tc) recognize and kill virally-infected cells.

time they acquire new molecules encoded by the virus. A group of large, granular lymphocytes recognize these changes and are able to kill the infected cell. This function is called natural killer cell action and the lymphocytes that carry it out are termed NK cells (see Box 2.4).

BOX 2.4   T cells, B cells and NK cells

There are two principal groups of lymphocytes responsible for recognizing antigens: **B cells**, which differentiate in the bone marrow, and **T cells**, which develop in the thymus gland, overlying the heart. B cells have a surface antibody as a receptor to recognize *intact* antigens, either in body fluids or on the surface of other cells. Activated B cells go on to produce a secreted form of their own surface antibody. T cells, in contrast, recognize antigen *fragments* that are presented on the cell surface, and they perform numerous roles in immune responses. Large, granular lymphocytes, which act as **NK cells**, are a distinct third population of lymphocyte.

The actions of interferons and NK cells both occur early in an immune response, and are not specific for the flu virus – these defences occur in response to many different kinds of viral infection, and they are part of our natural, or non-adaptive, immune responses. *Note: immunologists use the term non-adaptive to indicate a type of response that does not improve or adapt with each subsequent infection. This is quite different to its use in evolutionary biology, where it means 'not advantageous'.* Such non-adaptive immune responses slow the spread of an infection so that specific, or adaptive, immune defences can come into play.

The key features of an adaptive immune response are specificity and memory. The immune response is specific to a particular pathogen, and the immune system appears to 'remember' the infection, so that if it occurs again the immune response is much more powerful and rapid. Because an immune response is specific to a particular pathogen it often means that a response against one strain of virus will be ineffective against another – if a virus mutates then the lymphocytes that mediate adaptive immunity are unable to recognize the new strain.

There are two principal arms of the adaptive immune system, mediated by different populations of lymphocytes. One group, called T-lymphocytes, or T cells, recognizes antigens associated with cells of the body, including cells which have become infected. A set of cytotoxic T cells (Tc) specifically recognizes cells which have become infected and will go on to kill them. In this sense they act in a similar way to NK cells. However they differ from NK cells in that Tc cells are specific for one antigen or infectious agent, whereas NK cells are non-specific. The second group of lymphocytes are B cells, which synthesize antibodies that can recognize free virus, and lead to its uptake and destruction by phagocytic cells. Therefore the T cells and NK cells deal with the intracellular phase of the viral infection, while the B cells and antibodies recognize and deal with the extracellular virus.

You might ask why it takes the adaptive immune response so long to get going. The answer is that the number of T cells and B cells that recognize any specific pathogen is relatively small, so first the lymphocytes which specifically recognize the virus must divide so that there are sufficient to mount an effective immune response. This mechanism is fundamental to all adaptive immune responses.

Learning outcomes for Chapter 2

When you have studied this chapter, you should be able to:

2.1 Define and use, or recognise definitions and applications of, each of the terms printed in **bold** in the text.

2.2 Describe influenza viruses, their structure, how they are transmitted, how they infect cells and replicate and how they produce their damage in the host. (*Questions 2.2, 2.3 and 2.4*)

2.3 Outline the different types of immune defence which are deployed against flu infections, distinguishing those that act against infected cells from those that act against free virus. (*Question 2.4*)

2.4 Describe the differences between strains of virus. (*Questions 2.3 and 2.5*)

2.5 Describe how strains of the virus change over time, and relate this to the flu viruses that occur in birds and other mammals. (*Questions 2.3 and 2.5*)

2.6 Explain how the epidemic pattern of influenza can be related to the evolution of new strains of virus and to the specificity of the immune response against each strain. (*Question 2.5*)

Questions for Chapter 2

Question 2.1

Why would Robert Koch have been unable to demonstrate that influenza viruses cause the disease influenza, according to his own postulates?

Question 2.2

List the various structural components of an influenza-A virus and note where each of these elements is synthesised within an infected cell.

Question 2.3

It is very uncommon for a strain of influenza that infects other animals to infect people; nevertheless such strains are very important for human disease. Why is this?

Question 2.4

Which immune defences are able to recognise and destroy virally-infected host cells?

Question 2.5

Why do most people suffer from influenza several times in their lives?

3 MALARIA: A CASE STUDY

In this case study you will use a CD-ROM and the Internet to gather information about aspects of malaria. The main aims are to develop methods of searching for information and to get an overview of the disease. Indeed, as you will see, there is such a vast literature on the subject of malaria that it would be impossible to learn even a small fraction of it.

We are using three CDs from the Wellcome Trust in this course, on malaria, tuberculosis and HIV. They have been chosen because they are produced by international experts, the subject matter in each is clearly explained, and they provide examples of externally produced educational material on infectious disease. They may also be useful for your assessed work, and they provide extensive background reading.

There are three phases of study when using the CD or the Internet. The first is *exploration* in which you browse the material in an open-ended way. This gives you a feel for the range of material. The second is *familiarization and consolidation,* in which you become clearer about the structure and the broad content of the information (including the links, hierarchies of information and quality of information). Finally, you may wish to concentrate on particular aspects or questions and seek detailed information in a *focused* manner. These three phases are probably familiar to you from other study or from general use of the Internet.

3.1 The Malaria CD-ROM

Instructions for installing and accessing the CD material are given on the inside sleeve of the CD. If you follow these instructions it should take a maximum of 3–4 minutes to install and reboot. Once you have completed Step 4 select Interactive tutorials and then Overview.

3.1.1 Exploration

Start with a 15-minute exploration *within the overview*. On any page, you can click on ? at the top right to see explanations of all the features, and then click anywhere else to go back to the page. Use the arrow keys at the bottom right to move between pages. Try the find, glossary and reference facilities. Try using the notepad.

3.1.2 Familiarization

Now work through the first ten pages of the overview in a more systematic manner. Click on some of the hotspots on the map (i.e. the white spots on page 4) and follow the life cycle in humans and life cycle in mosquito graphics on page 7. Finally, try the questions at the end of this section, on page 11. We do not expect you to attempt familiarization with the other sections at this stage.

3.1.3 Focusing

There are many issues raised in the overview that we could focus on. Let us select one that comes up later in the course and that is highly topical — the search for a malaria vaccine.

Use find to get information from the overview about malaria vaccine. Click on find and enter the key word *vaccine* in the word/phrase box. Click on find (bottom right) within this window. This should direct you to information on pages 35 and 44. Go to those pages and read the information (double-clicking on the search entry should take you to the page).

On pages 35 and 44 you will see that there is 'currently no recommended vaccine for malaria'. Three approaches to vaccine development are also shown on page 35. Your understanding of these approaches will become clearer as you progress through the course, although you should be able to understand the principles by cross-referencing with the life cycle graphics in the overview.

An important word here is *currently* — like so much of the infectious disease material, vaccine development is a rapidly moving field and parts of the CD may be out of date (hopefully not by too much!). You can see how recent the source material is by clicking on references.

○ What are the most recent references relevant to malaria vaccines?

● A year 2000 reference on page 35 (which contains several references to malaria vaccine development).

In order to check on the latest situation you will need to use the Internet. Close the CD by clicking on the × in the top right (you may have to do this for several pages).

3.2 Web searches for malaria vaccine

You may be undertaking your searches one or more years after this case study is written. We therefore expect that some of the websites may have changed, and that the information may have been updated. Thus you may be able to add further information to that provided by the links we have identified. We plan to post any important changes to links on the S320 course website.

The three phases of study on the Internet will be as identified for the CD.

3.2.1 Exploration

Begin with an open search using your current search engine and the search term 'malaria vaccine'. Open up a few of the web sites identified as most relevant. Archive any potentially useful ones by adding to your Favorites (or similar); it is helpful to set up a folder for these. Note that you are looking for recent studies (after the publication of the CD, i.e. post 2000), so check when the site was last updated. You should also look out for the reliability of the sources. Personal websites, or those without clear academic or organizational affiliations, may not be reliable.

3.2.2 Familiarization

Go back to two of the websites you identified where there is some detail on the search for a vaccine. If you wish, you can try web sites that we have identified (see the *Resources* section on the course website). Make some brief notes on the latest situation, who is doing the work, and where.

Suggested links

The World Health Organization (WHO) has a wide range of useful information. The home page covers recent health stories, including infectious disease, with full text access. The WHO malaria link page can be found by clicking on Health Topics (A to Z) in the left-hand side menu of the home page. The Malaria Fact Sheet (no. 94) has links to various aspects of malaria, including 'Developing New Anti-Malarial Drugs'. At March 2002 this stated that the 'search for a vaccine continues' and that 'more than a dozen candidate vaccines are currently in development'.

The WHO sponsors organizations such as the Special Programme for Research and Training in Tropical Diseases (TDR), whose mission is to focus on neglected infectious diseases that disproportionately affect poor and marginalized populations (covering ten diseases including malaria). Searching on the key words *malaria vaccine* in the searchable WHO website gave us 1250 hits, including Final Report 33 (click on Download pdf; updated July 2001), which stated that an antigen was ready to proceed to vaccine trials in primates . Clicking on this report takes you to TDR research.

3.2.3 Focusing

Now follow up one of the suggested latest areas of research. When we were preparing this activity a Reuters news article was found, dated Dec 17, 2001, which stated that 'genetically engineered mice have produced a malaria vaccine in their milk that worked to protect monkeys from the disease'. It also mentioned that, if the trials were successful, goats could become production centres for the vaccine. You can read the Reuters article or follow up one you have found. The work was undertaken by Stowers, Miller and others at the National Institute of Allergy and Infectious Disease (NIAID). The NIAID website is comprehensive and includes the original press release that prompted the Reuters article. This, along with the Reuters article, stated that the work was being published in Proceedings of the National Academy of Science (PNAS). This was our lead to look at the primary literature, to see where the original research was first published.

3.3 Accessing the primary literature

We have found that the original scientific study (the primary source) was published in PNAS. If you go to the PNAS website you will find a search engine that allows you to look at abstracts (summaries) or the full text of articles published since 1966.

Search on the key terms 'malaria vaccine' in the abstract and title. Limit the search to articles about one year old. In our case we searched from January 2001 to July

2002 and came up with 72 articles, which included the Stowers *et al.* article, which was published in January 2002. The reference for this article is:

Stowers, A. W. *et al.* (2002) A recombinant vaccine expressed in the milk of transgenic mice protects Aotus monkeys from a lethal challenge with *Plasmodium falciparum*, *Proceedings of the National Academy of Science,* **99**, pp. 339–344.

The full article is quite complex but the final message from the abstract is clear: 'This study demonstrates the potential for producing efficacious malarial vaccines in transgenic animals'. You may like to archive this document for reference once you have studied S320 Book 7.

You should be able to use these techniques of searching on the CDs and the Internet to gather information for your assessed work and to explore the latest issues in infectious disease.

Learning outcomes for Chapter 3

When you have studied this chapter, you should be able to:

3.1   Demonstrate familiarity with the format and structure of the Wellcome Trust CD.

3.2   Search for malaria information on the Internet.

3.3   Access abstracts of a scientific journal (primary literature).

4 HOSPITAL ACQUIRED INFECTIONS: A CASE STUDY

This final chapter in Book 1 is a case study of a particular source of infection – hospitals. It also introduces several topics that are taught in later books in the course and reinforces material from earlier chapters.

4.1 Hospitals as sources of infection

Infirmaries, or hospitals, in all countries, are for the most part unclean and infectious places, and tho' every precaution is taken to purify them … the seeds of infection once sown, continue, in some instances, to spread contagious diseases, and to contaminate the house.

(Sir Richard Brocklesby, 1764, Physician-General of the British Army, from his *Oeconomical and Medical Observations*, quoted in Selwyn, 1991)

… although the establishment of hospitals is a necessity … the bringing together within a confined area of many sick persons is perilous. The risks of contamination of the air and of impregnation of the material of the building with morbid substances, are so greatly increased, that the greatest care is necessary that hospitals should not become pesthouses, and do more harm than good.

(Sir James Young Simpson, 1867, physician to Queen Victoria in Scotland, from his address 'On Public Health', quoted in Selwyn, 1991)

Hospital acquired infections are a huge problem for the National Health Service. They prolong patients' stay in hospital and, in the worst cases, cause permanent disability and even death.

(Sir John Bourne, 2000, Comptroller and Auditor General, from his report to the UK Parliament, quoted in National Audit Office, 2000a)

The similarity of these observations, spanning more than two centuries, reminds us that the most modern hospitals in the richest countries on earth – like the institutions that preceded them – remain 'perilous' for some of their patients. Diseases or disabilities caused by medical procedures are known as **iatrogenic illnesses** (from the Greek *iatros*, physician), and they include the side effects of drugs or medical radiation, unintended damage resulting from surgery, and infections acquired in hospitals. This chapter gives an overview of hospital infections, and explores the reasons for their persistence throughout the history of hospitalization, despite, and increasingly because of, medical progress.

4.1.1 Hospital acquired and nosocomial infections

A **hospital acquired infection**, or **HAI**, is any infection developed by a patient that was not present when he or she was admitted to the hospital, regardless of the causative agent. The majority of HAIs now, as in the past, are due to *bacteria*, but viruses, fungi and parasites are also significant causes 'in all countries', just as

Brocklesby observed in 1764. (You may encounter a broader translation of HAI as 'health-care associated infection', encompassing infections arising from any health-care activity wherever it occurs, for example in GP surgeries, residential care or domestic homes. But our focus here is on *hospitals* as sources of infection.)

Any communicable infection that is present in the community outside a hospital can be transmitted to patients and staff, who may then pass it on to others within the institution, an event termed **cross-infection**. Epidemic infections including influenza, HIV, tuberculosis, malaria and measles (among many others) are frequently transmitted to hospital patients, and not just in today's developing countries. In March 1999, a hospital in England reported three cases of hospital-acquired malaria, one of them fatal; the parasites are believed to have been transmitted in intravenous tubing, contaminated during treatment of other patients with malaria in an infectious diseases unit (CDR Weekly Report, 1999). This example illustrates the potential for cross-infection to occur even in a modern hospital unit specializing in treating serious infections.

In wealthy countries, where infectious disease is not a major cause of mortality *outside* hospitals, the majority of HAIs are caused by infectious agents that originated *within* the hospital. These HAIs are caused by pathogens that are rare outside health-care institutions (except in recently discharged patients), or that were introduced into the patient's body by a medical procedure. Research publications, particularly those from the USA, often use the term **nosocomial infections** (derived from the Latin *nosocomialis,* originating in hospital) to indicate this restricted focus. It is well worth using HAI and nosocomial as 'search terms' if you want to pursue this subject further via Internet searches. Later in the chapter we consider recent evidence about the extent of HAIs in modern Western hospitals and their consequences for patients and health services. But first we offer a glimpse into the long and shocking history of hospital infections.

4.1.2 Surgical gangrene and hospital fevers

From archaeological evidence and contemporary writings, the hospitals of antiquity, founded first in India, Sri Lanka, Egypt, Palestine and Greece, seem to have been spacious and well ventilated. Their medical attendants were selected partly for their cleanliness, and patients followed regimens of ritual purification. But, according to a history of hospital infection by Sydney Selwyn, a 'disastrous deterioration in European hygiene' occurred from about the fourth century AD, as a consequence of early Christian teaching about the body (Selwyn, 1991). St Jerome's dictum that 'he who has washed in Christ need never wash again' exemplifies the medieval Christian belief, prevailing in Europe until at least the sixteenth century, that the 'mortification of the flesh' and the subjugation of the body was essential in the service of the soul.

The religious orders that founded the great hospitals and infirmaries of medieval and Renaissance Europe considered the body to be a site of putrefaction, which could not be further corrupted in sickness even if patients lay crowded together in the filth of vast squalid wards. Suppuration (the production of pus) from wounds was considered essential for healing. Death was a constant presence (Figure 4.1). Even in the eighteenth century, it was common for up to six patients to share a bed in large municipal hospitals, and surgical procedures still took place in the open wards. The mortality rates among hospital patients were horrific, frequently exceeding 80%, as infectious diseases spread through the wards like wildfire. Until the last quarter of the nineteenth century, to be committed to a hospital was feared by the general population as a death sentence. The risk to patients was a source of anguish to conscientious doctors, for example the Edinburgh surgeon John Bell, who advised his professional colleagues:

> … that without the circle of the infected walls the men are safe; let him, therefore, hurry them out of this house of death … let him lay them in a schoolroom, a church, on a dunghill or in a stable … let him carry them anywhere but to their graves.
>
> (Bell, J., 1801, *The Principles of Surgery*, Volume 1; quoted in Selwyn, 1991)

Until the first major period of hospital reform began in Europe in the 1860s, it is highly probable that most patients acquired an infection while in hospital. The patients at most risk were those with open fractures, abdominal wounds, or who required surgery for any reason, and women after childbirth. The medical historian Roy Porter quotes a study from the 1840s, which found that deaths from puerperal or 'childbed' fever reached 29% in the largest maternity clinic in the world, the Vienna General Hospital (Porter, 1997). The principal causative agent was infection with the bacterium *Streptococcus pyogenes*.

Post-operative mortality from 'surgical gangrene' (also predominantly due to streptococcal bacteria) could be as high as 80% in some European hospitals in the nineteenth century, between three and five times greater than for surgery performed in domestic houses. Dressings and plasters were re-used time and again; staff did not wash their hands between attending to one patient and the next; surgical instruments were 'wiped clean' and surgeons operated in their street clothes, or worse, as in this example recalled by a medical student in a Leeds hospital in the 1880s:

FIGURE 4.1
Depiction of a seventeenth-century hospital ward in a treatise published in 1688 in Amsterdam. In the foreground a physician inspects a urine sample, while a post-mortem dissection is carried out in the open ward by doctors in their 'street' clothes, including hats and wigs. In the background, two bodies are being loaded into coffins.

> He rolled up his shirt-sleeves and, in the corridor to the operation room, he took an ancient frock from a cupboard; it bore signs of a chequered past, and was utterly stiff with old blood. One of these coats was worn with special pride, indeed joy, as it had belonged to a retired member of the staff.
>
> (Quoted in Porter, 1997)

In addition to puerperal fever, other fatal 'hospital fevers' were also very common, caused by a variety of pathogens. One of these was certainly typhus transmitted by body lice in infected bedding; others may have been due to malaria or influenza, or to bloodstream infections (septicaemia) from infected wounds. Not until the successful use of carbolic acid as an antiseptic was published by Joseph Lister in 1867 did surgical and maternal mortality rates begin to fall, and then only in those places where Pasteur's bacterial theory of infection was accepted (modern antiseptics are discussed further in Book 7). But as the 'sanitarian' movement gathered pace, hospital reformers such as Florence Nightingale raised standards of cleanliness in hospital premises and introduced hygienic methods to reduce cross-infection between staff and patients. By the end of the nineteenth century, these measures had begun to control **pyogenic** (pus-forming) infections in surgical wards and maternity units, and the focus of concern had shifted to respiratory infections in medical wards, particularly among children.

As children's wards became established in major hospitals towards the end of the nineteenth century, child patients suffered considerable mortality and morbidity from hospital-acquired fevers due to measles, whooping cough, diphtheria, scarlet fever and other infections of the throat and respiratory system. Although measures such as spacing beds more widely and increasing the flow of air through the wards produced some reduction in airborne cross-infection, HAIs still posed a significant risk to children's health until at least the 1950s.

○ What reduced the threat of fatal infectious disease among children in Britain from the 1950s onwards (recall Chapter 1)?

● Routine vaccinations for a number of important childhood infections were introduced at around that time, including whooping cough, diphtheria and tuberculosis; also, death rates fell as antibiotics became more widely used, for example to treat diphtheria and scarlet fever.

The extent of HAIs in children's wards can be judged from a study conducted by the medical bacteriologist Joyce Wright, into their incidence in University College Hospital, London, in 1937, a decade before the inception of the NHS (Wright, 1940). In these wards, precautions to avoid cross-infection were extensive and included taking a throat swab from every child on admission and maintaining isolation from other patients until a negative result was confirmed for the major bacterial pathogens. Yet despite these measures, in that year a total of 104 children (19% of all admissions) became infected during their stay and three died; 72 children, 8 nurses and a ward maid became infected with *Streptococcus* bacteria resulting (variously) in sore throats, wound suppuration, ear infections and fever; one child caught measles and 15 caught diphtheria; 16 children and one nurse suffered dysentery or gastro-enteritis; and one child and three nurses were diagnosed with 'catarrhal jaundice' with acute fever. Studies such as these remind us that within living memory, even in the most highly regarded hospitals, children's wards were major sources of infection (Figure 4.2), and that staff were also at risk.

Although the threat of death from HAIs in Western hospitals fell rapidly during the second half of the twentieth century, fatalities still occur and HAIs remain a significant cause of morbidity, as the quotation from the Auditor General at the start of this chapter testifies. The most recent national prevalence survey of HAIs in England found that around 9% of all patients admitted to an acute (short-stay) hospital acquired an infection from other patients, hospital staff, contaminated equipment, the premises, the water supply or the food (National Audit Office, 2000b). These infections are estimated to contribute to around 1000 deaths every year; on average a patient who acquires an infection in an English hospital is seven times more likely to die during that admission than an equivalent patient who remains uninfected (Plowman *et al.*, 2000).

FIGURE 4.2
Child patients on the balcony of a children's ward at St Thomas's Hospital in London in the 1940s, within sight of the Houses of Parliament and 'Big Ben'. At this date, up to 20% of children in metropolitan hospitals acquired an infection after admission.

Later in this chapter we review the recent epidemiology of HAIs, but first some reflections on what makes even a modern hospital a 'high risk' site for acquiring an infection. In many respects, the hazards are exactly the same as those of the past, but although advances in medical technology have decreased some infection risks they have, paradoxically, created new opportunities for hospital patients to acquire an infection.

4.1.3 Infection risks in modern hospitals

Infectious diseases that occur in the population outside a hospital frequently spread more rapidly within it.

○ Why are hospital patients likely to be more susceptible to infection?

● People who are ill tend to have less effective immune responses against infection, particularly if they are very young or very old (a point made in Chapter 2, see discussion of Figure 2.3; Book 3 explains the mechanisms underlying this deficiency); people in these age groups are also more likely to be hospitalized if they are ill, so they make up a larger proportion of patients than occurs in the community outside. Surgical patients and people with traumatic injuries are particularly at risk because wounds expose tissues on which pathogens rapidly proliferate. Some patients are more vulnerable to infection because they are taking drugs to suppress their immune responses, for example to prevent organ transplant rejection; cancer chemotherapy and some other drugs also have the unwanted side-effect of reducing immunity.

Suppressed immunity not only increases susceptibility to common infectious diseases, it also allows the proliferation of so-called **opportunistic infections**, which can only develop in people whose immune system is deficient. Other factors that increase vulnerability are behavioural: for example, maintaining personal hygiene may be difficult for people who are frail or ill or taking psychoactive drugs, and low physical activity increases the risk of a respiratory infection gaining a hold in poorly ventilated lungs.

○ Which features of hospitals make infection control particularly difficult? Think about the structure and functions of hospital premises and equipment.

● Hospitals consist of wards, offices, operating theatres, specialist therapy or diagnostic units, laboratories, dispensaries, etc., all of which are routinely exposed to sources of infection and are difficult to clean thoroughly. Some areas pose a particular cleaning problem because they are in constant use (e.g. wards, accident and emergency (A&E) departments, intensive care units). Hospitals also usually have an industrial-scale kitchen, a laundry, water storage tanks, mountains of waste for disposal that includes contaminated instruments and dressings, and a sewerage system that must deal with all kinds of body fluids including blood. They are full of complex technical equipment and instruments, which can be hard to sterilize, and which touch or enter the body of people who are already ill. Last but not least, patients are housed in close proximity to each other and must share eating, washing and toilet facilities, which makes cross-infection much more likely.

The hospital water supply can harbour pathogens in the storage tanks, in the miles of plumbing connecting hundreds of sinks, baths, showers and toilets, and in the cooling towers serving the central heating system and laundry. Cases of hospital-acquired legionnaires' disease (caused by the bacterium *Legionella pneumophila*) have been traced to water droplets descending as an aerosol from hospital cooling towers and shower heads, but the commonest source of *Legionella* infection is from water used to 'humidify' the airways of patients on respirators or nebulizers. Airborne dust particles are another carrier of respiratory HAIs, and many outbreaks of food-borne infections have occurred as a result of failures in safety standards in hospital kitchens. But the most significant agents of HAIs are still the 'traditional' sources – the people who touch patients and the equipment used in medical procedures.

Unless strict precautions are taken, hospital staff who move from one patient to another in quick succession can readily transfer pathogens from person-to-person on their hands, clothing or equipment. In the eighteenth century, the hands of doctors and midwives were found to be the transmitters of puerperal fever, and inadequate hand hygiene remains an important source of cross-infection today. HAIs can also be transmitted by articles as diverse and as apparently innocuous as stethoscopes, rinse-and-spit mouth wash, and the neck ties worn by male doctors! Stethoscopes and neckties are examples of **fomites**, a collective term for any inanimate object that acts as a vehicle for transmitting pathogens between people.

The highest risk of acquiring an infection in hospitals occurs in areas where patients are in contact with the most complex fomites of all: the equipment used to maintain life-support in intensive care units (ICUs) and special-care baby units (or paediatric ICUs, Figure 4.3). Operating theatres, surgical wards and kidney dialysis units are also key sites of transmission for HAIs. In these settings, patients are routinely hooked up to equipment via plastic tubing delivering fluids, drugs and nutrition, or draining body fluids from the chest cavity, abdomen, bladder or a surgical wound. Tubing may be connected to a hollow needle inserted in a blood vessel (an intravenous or IV line), or passing up the nose and down the oesophagus into the stomach (naso-gastric tube). During dialysis for people with kidney failure, the patient's blood supply is routed out of the body three or four times a week and passed along semi-permeable polymer tubes through a device that draws

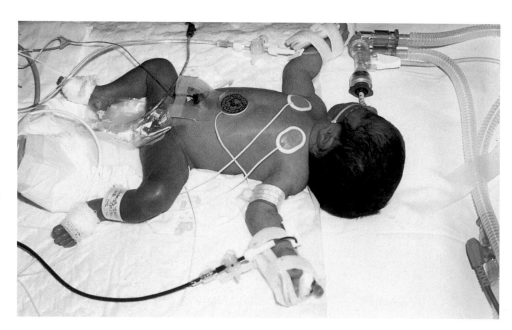

FIGURE 4.3
Premature babies in special-care paediatric units are at risk from HAIs transmitted via medical equipment. This baby is attached to a ventilator to maintain respiration, intravenous lines in blood vessels in both arms deliver antibiotics and nutritional supplements, sensors attached to the baby's chest and abdomen monitor heart beat and lung movement, and urine is drained from the bladder via a catheter.

impurities out of the blood, before returning it to the patient.

Medical tubing forms an ideal substrate for bacterial and fungal pathogens, which settle on the surface and proliferate to form a sheet known as a **biofilm** (Figure 4.4). Tubing, including catheters draining urine from the bladder, may have to stay in place for several days at a time, and the longer they are in position the greater the risk of infection. The respiratory system is a vulnerable site for people undergoing a general anaesthetic, which requires the patient to be attached to a mechanical ventilator via a tube inserted into the trachea (windpipe). People on life-support systems in ICUs may have to be ventilated for several weeks.

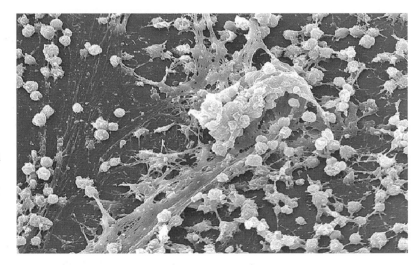

10 μm

Figure 4.5 shows the proportion of **bacteraemias** (bloodstream infections caused by bacteria) arising from the major routes of entry into the body.

FIGURE 4.4
A biofilm is formed when microbes adhere irreversibly to an inanimate surface by secreting a sticky matrix of polysaccharides. Here a biofilm of *Staphylococcus* bacteria has formed on the inner surface of a plastic connector used to join medical tubing.

○ What conclusions can be drawn from Figure 4.5 about the relative risks of bacteraemia arising from different medical procedures?

◖ The greatest risk is associated with the use of a central intravenous catheter (an 'IV line' inserted into a central blood vessel), which, together with catheters in peripheral blood vessels and the urinary tract, accounts for almost half of all bacteraemias. Five per cent begin as surgical site infections, but the source of over a quarter of bacteraemias is unknown.

unknown (27%)

central IV catheter (31%)

other (2%)

skin & soft tissue (3%)

intra-abdominal (3%)

catheter-associated UTI (9%)

non-catheter-associated UTI (3%)

gastrointestinal tract (4%)

ventilator-associated RTI (2%)

non-ventilator-associated RTI (4%)

surgical site infection (5%)

peripheral IV catheter (7%)

FIGURE 4.5
Proportion of hospital-acquired bacteraemias in English hospitals surveyed between 1997 and 1999, according to the route of entry into the body. IV, intravenous; UTI, urinary tract infection; RTI, respiratory tract infection.

Thus HAIs should be seen as having multiple interacting 'causes'. One set of factors arise from the nature of the pathogens themselves (e.g. the ability to form biofilms), but their impact on hospital patients is also a consequence of the enhanced susceptibility to infection of people who are ill, and also to the structure and organization of health-care institutions, the behaviour of their staff and the complexity of medical equipment, particularly if it penetrates the body. In the next section, we review the epidemiology of HAIs, the pathogens that cause most concern as sources of HAIs in health-care settings, and the types of infection they cause.

Summary of Section 4.1

1 A hospital acquired infection (HAI) is any infection in a patient that was not present when he or she was admitted to the hospital.

2 Until the end of the nineteenth century, epidemic diseases, gangrene and fevers caused huge mortality in European hospitals; post-operative death rates exceeded 80% in some places and puerperal fever killed up to 30% of women in childbirth.

3 In the early twentieth century, HAIs due to pyogenic infections began to decline as antiseptic techniques and antibiotic drugs became widespread, and attention switched to controlling respiratory HAIs, particularly in children's wards.

4 By the end of the twentieth century, 9% of patients in English hospitals acquired an infection during their admission, and HAIs contributed to an estimated 1000 deaths annually.

5 The agents that cause HAIs are transmitted on the hands of health workers, via fomites such as clothing, stethoscopes and (increasingly) life-support equipment and medical tubing in which bacterial and fungal pathogens can adhere as a biofilm. HAIs are also transmitted in airborne dust particles and water droplets and in hospital food.

4.2 The epidemiology of HAIs

Although HAIs have been identified as a significant health problem for more than two centuries, reliable data on the incidence of these infections remain patchy and incomplete. Comparisons between places and over time are hampered by the lack of routine data collection and inconsistencies in the ways in which data have been collected; for example, studies may use different detection methods to identify infectious agents, or survey different categories of patients. So at the start of the twenty-first century it is difficult to conclude whether (and if so where), the control of HAIs is getting better or getting worse. Until *longitudinal* studies (as described in Chapter 1) are conducted using consistent methods repeated at intervals over a significant period of time, we must rely on *cross-sectional* data that offer 'snapshots' of the situation at a particular time and place.

The inadequacy of epidemiological data on HAIs in England began to be addressed in 1996, when the Department of Health and the Public Health Laboratory Service established the Nosocomial Infection National Surveillance Scheme (NINSS), to standardize the collection of information about infections acquired in hospitals. The first reports on HAIs based on NINSS results were published between 2000 and

2002 (and are cited below); these are the most recent sources available for any part of the UK at the time of writing this chapter.

4.2.1 Microbes involved in HAIs

The biology of many of the pathogenic microbes involved in HAIs is discussed in Book 2, which also explains the conventions on bacterial nomenclature and the use of italics. Here, our aim is simply to illustrate the point that the range of pathogens involved in HAIs is very large and to note that the majority are bacteria. The distribution of HAIs by 'main site' in the body is shown in Figure 4.6.

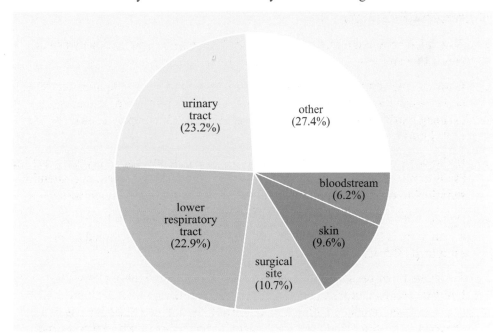

FIGURE 4.6 The distribution of HAIs by site in the body, based on a survey of 37 111 patients in 15 hospitals in England between May 1993 and July 1994. At any one time, it was calculated that a mean of 9% of hospital inpatients were affected by an HAI.

Urinary tract infections (UTIs) are the most common infection acquired in hospitals, and patients with in-dwelling catheters draining the bladder are at greatest risk. Significant bacterial causes of UTIs are *Enterococcus* species and *Chlamydia trachomatis*, and the yeast *Candida albicans* (which causes 'thrush') is also widespread. Respiratory infections are the second most prevalent category of HAIs, with bacterial, viral and fungal causes. *Streptococcus pneumoniae* is the major bacterial agent, but *Chlamydia pneumoniae* and several viruses including influenza virus, rhinovirus and respiratory syncitial virus (RSV, the leading cause of HAIs in special-care baby units) are important respiratory pathogens.

Although urinary tract and lower respiratory tract infections are the most common categories of HAI, bacteraemias have the highest mortality rates and **surgical site infections** (affecting surgical wounds) are among the most difficult to treat. Two studies using NINSS data from English hospitals focused on these categories of HAI. A total of 61 hospitals participated in the bacteraemia survey, reporting 3824 episodes – a rate of 3.6 patients affected per 1000 admissions. A total of 1212 surgical site infections were reported by 96 hospitals; the surgical procedures in which wounds were most likely to become infected were limb amputations

(14.5% infected) and large bowel surgery (10.4% infected). Table 4.1 shows the pathogens most commonly involved.

TABLE 4.1 Pathogens most commonly causing bacteraemias or surgical site infections in patients in English hospitals, 1997–1999.

Pathogen	Bacteraemias due to this pathogen (%)	Surgical site infections due to this pathogen (%)
Staphylococcus aureus	24	38
coagulase-negative staphylococci	20	9
Escherichia coli	13	3
Enterococcus species	8	7
Enterobacter species	5	2
Pseudomonas aeruginosa	3	5
Streptococcus species	1	5
others	26	31

The most obvious conclusion to be drawn from Table 4.1 is that staphylococci are the most important bacterial cause of HAIs, a finding that is confirmed in the hospitals of other developed nations. Staphylococci are normally present on the skin and most species do no harm, but a few cause skin infections and they can be a serious problem in hospitals. *Staphylococcus aureus* is unusual in producing an enzyme called coagulase; other staphylococci are referred to collectively as coagulase-negative. The greatest media publicity concerning infection of surgical wounds has been generated by the old enemy *Streptococcus pyogenes*, which has been dubbed the 'flesh-eating bacteria' of tabloid headlines; in the post-antibiotic era this outcome is a rare complication of surgical site infections with this bacterium.

Before turning to what undoubtedly *is* the major concern about HAIs in the twenty-first century, it is worth noting that the systematic collection of data in the hospitals of Western industrialized nations is a relatively recent initiative. Evidence from developing countries is much more fragmentary, and localized to small-scale studies in individual hospitals and clinics. However, the prevalence of infectious diseases in the general populations of the developing world, coupled with the very low levels of funding for health care, lead to the inexorable conclusion that the problem of HAIs must be many times worse than the situation reported here for England. The pathogens named above are far from a complete list of those involved in HAIs, and the range is much greater in poor countries, or in areas of rapid political change (e.g. South Africa, the former Soviet Union). Moreover, in many parts of the developing world, a high proportion of hospital patients is already immunodeficient as a result of infection with HIV and/or tuberculosis (Figure 4.7); these patients readily acquire opportunistic and other infections in hospitals.

4.2.2 Drug resistance and HAIs

An emerging problem with HAIs in the developed world is that they are increasingly due to **drug-resistant strains**: pathogens that have evolved the ability to survive exposure to the drugs most frequently used to treat them. (The mechanisms by which drug resistance evolves and spreads are described in Book 2.) The widespread *prophylactic* use of antibiotics in hospitals to prevent the development of bacterial infections in vulnerable patients (e.g. those on life-support systems in ICUs), has been one selection pressure in the development of increasingly drug-resistant strains. The profligacy with which antibiotics were prescribed for minor infections in the community until the mid-1990s has been another driving force, as has the routine use of similar antibiotic compounds in animal husbandry. Bacterial drug resistance has also been rising in many developing countries, where even injectable antibiotics and syringes are widely sold to the public from market stalls and unlicensed drug stores at a lower cost than a doctor would charge.

The most important examples of antibiotic drug resistance can be understood by reference to the bacteria listed earlier in Table 4.1. The survey of English hospitals reported in Table 4.1, which identified *Staphylococcus aureus* as the most prevalent cause of surgical site infections, also found that a staggering 61% of cases were resistant to the previously most effective antibiotic, methicillin. Methicillin-resistant *Staphylococcus aureus*, or **MRSA**, can result in persistent wound infections causing deep tissue damage (Figure 4.8). The incidence of new cases has been growing rapidly in recent years, particularly in the UK, the USA (see Table 4.2) and other parts of the developed world. The importance of maintaining effective antibiotics against staphylococcal bacteria is underlined by the failure of repeated attempts throughout the twentieth century to develop a vaccine to protect high-risk patients.

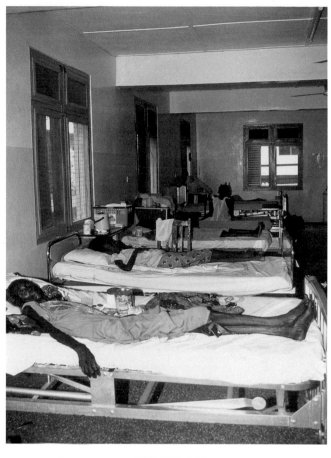

FIGURE 4.7
HIV, the human immunodeficiency virus, greatly increases susceptibility to other infections. There is a high risk of cross-infection between patients with HIV-related illnesses, as in this ward in a modern teaching hospital in Ghana.

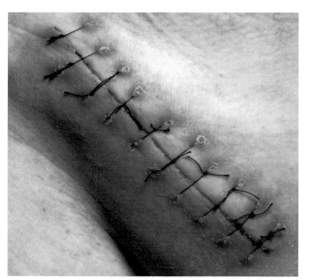

FIGURE 4.8
The inflammation and 'crusting' of dried pus around the stitches closing this surgical wound are typical signs of post-operative hospital acquired infection. The rapid increase in antibiotic resistance among bacterial species that commonly infect surgical sites is a growing cause for concern in Western hospitals.

TABLE 4.2 Antibiotic resistance in some bacterial pathogens causing HAIs in patients treated in ICUs in the USA: rates in 1999 compared with mean rate of resistance over previous 5 years.

Bacterial pathogen	Antibiotic	Bacterial isolates resistant in 1999 (%)	Change in resistance compared with 1994–1998 (%)
coagulase-negative staphylococci	methicillin	87.5	+2
Staphylococcus aureus	methicillin	52.3	+37
Enterobacter species	CCC*	34	−4
Enterococcus species	vancomycin	25.2	+43
Pseudomonas aeruginosa	quinolone	23.2	+50
Pseudomonas aeruginosa	CCC	23.2	+10
Pseudomonas aeruginosa	imipenem	21.4	+56

*CCC, resistance to one of ceftriaxone, cefotaxime or ceftazidime.

Surgical site infections are less commonly due to *Enterococcus* species, but these have also increasingly been found to resist treatment with the 'first choice' antibiotic, vancomycin. **VRE** (vancomycin-resistant *E. faecalis* or *E. faecium*) was first identified in Japan in the early 1990s, and has increased at an alarming rate in hospitals in the USA in recent years (Table 4.2), with isolated outbreaks beginning to appear in Europe. Vancomycin resistance has also been detected in strains of *Staphylococcus aureus* (VRSA).

Patients on ventilators are at particularly high risk of infection with *Pseudomonas aeruginosa*, which also commonly colonizes burns and other skin lesions.

○ Summarize the main features of the data in Table 4.2.

● In 1999 the majority of staphylococci isolated from ICUs in American hospitals were resistant to the principal antibiotics used to treat them. The proportion of MRSA had increased by over one third compared with the previous five-year average. Even larger increases were recorded for VRE and for quinolone-resistant *Pseudomonas aeruginosa*. Over one fifth of *P. aeruginosa* isolates were resistant to at least one of five different antibiotics normally used to treat this infection. *Enterobacter* species were the only category in which resistance had not increased, but one third of all isolates from ICUs were already resistant by 1999.

These data suggest that HAIs are likely to become more rather than less prevalent in Western hospitals in the future, and lead us to conclude this case study by considering the impact of HAIs on mortality and morbidity and the consequences for health service costs.

Summary of Section 4.2

1   Epidemiological data on HAIs in Britain have only been systematically collected since 1996; data from many countries, particularly in the developing world, are fragmentary, making it difficult to discern trends and make comparisons.

2   In English hospitals, the majority of HAIs are bacterial in origin and involve a wide range of bacterial species, but viral and fungal pathogens are also important.

3   Urinary tract and respiratory infections are the most common site for HAIs; bacteraemias and surgical site infections are more likely to end in fatality or long term damage, and in both these categories almost half of all cases are due to *Staphylococcus* species.

4   Antibiotic resistance is a growing problem in HAIs, with rates of 25–85% reported for some important pathogens (e.g. MRSA, VRE) in Western hospitals.

4.3 The costs of HAIs

The UK has a particularly poor track record for HAIs compared with other northern European countries, such as Iceland, Sweden, Denmark, Germany and the Netherlands. Of most concern in the UK is the rate of MRSA, which the European Antimicrobial Resistance Surveillance System detected in 46% of all isolates of this bacterium in British hospitals, the highest rate for any European country (*BMJ*, 2002). A north–south divide is apparent in Europe, with southern countries such as Italy and Greece generally presenting higher rates of HAIs than those in the north, but with the UK as the notable exception.

A major review of the socio-economic burden of HAIs in England (Plowman *et al.,* 2000) concluded that approximately 100 000 people contracted an infection during a hospital stay each year, and that at any one time around 9% of all hospital patients were suffering from such an infection. HAIs were estimated to have:

• extended the period in hospital of these patients by, on average, 14 days;

• contributed to an estimated 1000 deaths a year;

• cost the National Health Service close to £1 billion a year;

• extended the period of convalescence by a total of 8.7 million days; and

• cost patients an estimated £4.74 million per year on prescription charges and over-the-counter expenses for drugs and dressings.

◯   What other economic or social costs must have been incurred as a result of HAIs?

⬤   There must also be significant costs to the national economy in terms of lost productivity, sickness benefits paid to patients and social security payments to support their dependents. The longer period spent in hospitals by people with HAIs 'blocks' beds that could have been occupied by other patients, who must wait longer for treatment. (The study by Plowman *et al.* calculated that even a 10% reduction in HAIs in English hospitals would release between 300 000 and 425 000 bed-days per year.) Family members or other informal carers give up their time to look after people who are convalescing after an HAI, possibly with detrimental effects on their own health or income.

The USA is another country where HAIs have increased significantly in recent years, affecting around 2 million people annually. The cost to the US health service has been estimated at $4.5 billion per year, and HAIs are implicated in at least

88 000 deaths annually – one every six minutes (Weinstein, 1998). By 2000, hospital-acquired bloodstream infections had become the eighth leading cause of death in the USA (Wenzel and Edmond, 2001). Studies in New York teaching hospitals have shown that for patients who are infected with *Staphylococcus aureus*, the average period of inpatient stay, the death rate, and the cost per patient are all approximately double the rate experienced by equivalent but uninfected patients (Rubin *et al.*, 1999). Each case resulted in additional medical costs of close to $30 000. The costs of HAIs to individual hospitals can be gauged from this Australian example: a single outbreak of salmonella food poisoning in a Melbourne hospital resulted in additional costs equivalent to US $95 000 for medical care of patients, bacteriological investigations and lost productivity from staff who became ill (Spearing *et al.*, 2000).

○ Based on what you have read in this case study, what strategies do you think would be most effective in preventing the social and economic consequences of HAIs described above?

● The most important strategies involve better infection-control measures within hospitals, particularly facilities and training to improve hand hygiene among health-care workers; more effective sterilization of equipment that enters or touches the patient's body; more effective aseptic surgical techniques; better monitoring and control of the safety of food, air and water supplies; higher standards of cleanliness in hospital premises. Greater care should also be taken in the use of antibiotics to minimize the evolution of more strains of drug-resistant bacterial pathogens.

These precautions have self-evidently proved difficult to sustain in the most modern hospitals of wealthy economies. In developing countries where health service spending is severely constrained by weak economic performance, rapid population growth and natural disasters, it will be much harder to reduce the financial burden of HAIs on health systems. To put this point in context, consider what cross-infection control measures could be afforded in the hospitals of Bangladesh, where the total state funding for health care is less than US $5 per person per year.

Summary of Section 4.3

1   HAIs in Western industrialized nations result in huge financial costs to health services in terms of extended admissions, additional tests and treatments, and increased staffing requirements. National income is also adversely affected through lost productivity and increased sickness benefits.

2   In addition to the mortality and morbidity associated with HAIs, patients incur significant expenditure and delayed recovery; hospital waiting lists are extended because patients with HAIs 'block' beds; carers contribute their time and may lose income.

3   Measures to control HAIs effectively are likely to be beyond the health budgets of the world's poorest countries.

Learning outcomes for Chapter 4

When you have studied this chapter, you should be able to:

4.1 Define and use, or recognize definitions and applications of, each of the terms printed in **bold** in the text. (*Question 4.1*)

4.2 Discuss the forces driving the incidence of hospital acquired infections in the past and in modern hospitals, including the structure and functions of premises, the nature of high-risk treatments, the use of antibiotics, and the behaviour of health-care workers. (*Question 4.2*)

4.3 Describe the major categories and sites of infection associated with HAIs and give some examples of the pathogens involved and their relative importance, commenting on trends in drug resistance. (*Question 4.3*)

4.4 Summarize the socio-economic and human costs attributable to HAIs. (*Question 4.4*)

Questions for Chapter 4

Question 4.1

Give brief definitions of the following terms: pyogenic bacteria; bacteraemia; MRSA; fomite.

Question 4.2

What reasons can you suggest for the paradoxical observation that the incidence of HAIs in modern hospitals is partly a consequence of advances in medical technology?

Question 4.3

All categories of HAI have declined in importance in modern hospitals compared with their incidence in Europe before the twentieth century, but which has seen the most striking reduction and why? What pathogen was its cause and what category of HAI is it most commonly associated with today?

Question 4.4

It has been estimated that around 30% of HAIs in modern Western hospitals are preventable by increased hand hygiene and other measures. What saving would accrue to the NHS in England if this level of prevention were to be achieved?

REFERENCES

Chapter 1

Bryder, L. (1988) *Below the Magic Mountain: A Social History of Tuberculosis in Twentieth-Century Britain*, Oxford University Press, Oxford.

Burnet, M. (1962) *Natural History of Infectious Disease*, Cambridge University Press, Cambridge.

Centers for Disease Control and Prevention (1999) Achievements in Public Health, 1900–1996, *Morbidity and Mortality Weekly Report*, **48**, pp. 621–628.

Dobson, M. J. (1989) Mortality gradients and disease exchanges: comparisons from Old England and Colonial America, *Social History of Medicine*, **2**, pp. 259–297.

Epstein, P. (1999) Climate and health, *Science*, **285**, pp. 347–348.

Heyman, D. L, Rodier, G. R. and the WHO Operational Support Team to the Global Outbreak Alert and Response Network (2001) Hot spots in a wired world: WHO surveillance of emerging and re-emerging infectious diseases, *The Lancet Infectious Diseases*, **1**, pp. 345–353.

NHS Scotland (2001) *Health in Scotland 2000*, Scottish Environmental Health Department, Edinburgh.

Public Health Laboratory Service (2002) *CDR Weekly Report 12* http://www.phls.co.uk/publications/cdr/archive02/News/news0702.html#GI2001 [at September 2002].

Royal College of General Practitioners (2001) *Annual Report 2000: The Weekly Returns Service*, Birmingham Research Unit of the RCGP, Birmingham.

Sorsby, A. (1944) *Medicine and Mankind*, Watts and Co., London.

Taylor, L. H., Latham, S. M. and Woolhouse, M. E. J. (2001) Risk factors for human disease emergence, *Philosophical Transactions of the Royal Society of London B*, **356**, pp. 983–989.

Williams, B. G., Gouws, E., Boschi-Pinto, C., Bryce, J. and Dye, C. (2002) Estimates of world-wide distribution of child deaths from acute respiratory infections, *The Lancet Infectious Diseases*, **2**, pp. 25–32.

WHO (2002) *Scaling Up the Response to Infectious Disease*, World Health Organization, Geneva.

Chapter 2

Noymer, A. and Garenne, M. (2000) The 1918 influenza epidemic's effects on sex differentials in mortality in the United States, *Population Development Review*, **26**, pp. 565–581.

Chapter 4

BMJ (2002) European surveillance shows north-south divide in resistant bacteria, *British Medical Journal*, **324**, p. 697.

CDR Weekly Report (1999) Hospital-acquired malaria in Nottingham, *CDR Weekly*, **9**, No.14, PHLS Communicable Disease Surveillance Centre, London.

Emmerson, A. M., Enstone, J. E., Griffin, M., Kelsey, M. C. and Smyth, E. T. (1996) The second national prevalence survey of infection in hospitals – overview of results, *Journal of Hospital Infection*, **32**, pp. 175–190.

National Audit Office (2000a) *Press Notice 6/00*, NAO, London.

National Audit Office (2000b) *The Management and Control of Hospital Acquired Infection in Acute NHS Trusts in England*, HC 230 Session 1999–00, NAO, London.

NNIS ICU Report (1999) *Antimicrobial Resistance 1999*, Centers for Disease Control and Prevention, Division of Healthcare Quality Promotion, Atlanta, Georgia.

PHLS (2000a) *Surveillance of Hospital-Acquired Bacteraemia in English Hospitals 1997–1999*, Public Health Laboratory Service, London.

PHLS (2000b) *Surveillance of Surgical Site Infection in English Hospitals 1997–1999*, Public Health Laboratory Service, London.

Plowman, R., Graves, N., Griffin, M., Roberts, J. A., Swan, A. V., Cookson, B. D. and Taylor, L. (2000) *The Socio-economic Burden of Hospital Acquired Infection*, Public Health Laboratory Service, London http://www.doh.gov.uk/haicosts.htm [accessed September 2002].

Porter, R. (1997) *The Greatest Benefit to Mankind*, HarperCollins Publishers, London.

Rubin, R. J., Harrington, C. A., Poon, A., Dietrich, K., Greene, J. A. and Moiduddin, A. (1999) The economic impact of *Staphylococcus aureus* infection in New York city hospitals, *Emerging Infectious Diseases*, **5**, pp. 9–17.

Selwyn, S. (1991) Hospital infection: the first 2500 years, *Journal of Hospital Infection*, **18**, pp. 5–64.

Spearing, N. M., Jensen, A., McCall, B. J. Neill, A. S. and McCormack, J. G. (2000) Direct costs associated with a nosocomial outbreak of *Salmonella* infection: an ounce of prevention is worth a pound of cure, *American Journal of Infection Control*, **28**, pp. 54–57.

Weinstein, W. A. (1998) Nosocomial infection update, *Emerging Infectious Diseases*, **4**, pp. 416–420.

Wenzel, R. P. and Edmond, M. B. (2001) The impact of hospital-acquired bloodstream infections, *Emerging Infectious Diseases*, **7**, pp. 174–177.

Wright, J. (1940) Nosocomial infections in children's wards, *Journal of Hygiene*, **40**, pp. 647–672.

FURTHER SOURCES

Chapter 1

Diamond, J. (1998) *Guns, Germs and Steel: A Short History of Everybody for the Last 13,000 Years,* Vintage (paperback edition), Jonathan Cape, London.

Porter, R. (1997) *The Greatest Benefit to Mankind: A Medical History of Humanity from Antiquity to the Present,* HarperCollins Publishers, London.

Chapter 2

Male, D., Brostoff, J. and Roitt, I. (2001) Immunology Interactive 3.0, Mosby, Disc 2, Lecture 'Influenza'.

Webster, R.G. (2001) A molecular whodunit, (Discussion of the origins of pandemic strains of influenza-A), *Science,* **293**, pp. 1773–1775.

Chapter 4

Diamond, J. (1998) *Guns, Germs and Steel: A Short History of Everybody for the Last 13,000 Years,* Vintage (paperback edition), Jonathan Cape, London.

Porter, R. (1997) *The Greatest Benefit to Mankind: A Medical History of Humanity from Antiquity to the Present,* HarperCollins Publishers, London.

ANSWERS TO QUESTIONS

QUESTION 1.1

(a) TB, sleeping sickness and plague are zoonoses, which can be transmitted to humans under naturally occurring circumstances from other vertebrates, e.g. cattle, large 'game' animals such as antelope and buffalo, and rodents, including rats, gerbils and ground squirrels. However, TB has been all but eradicated from cattle herds and milk production in developed countries, and even in the developing world the main reservoir of TB infection is in humans. The bacteria are now most commonly passed directly from person to person, so although technically defined as a zoonosis since it can still be transmitted from cattle to humans, TB is on the borderline of the WHO definition. Malaria does not have a reservoir of infection in non-human vertebrates and thus is not a zoonosis.

(b) Malaria, sleeping sickness and plague are all vector-borne diseases transmitted from mammals to humans by insects, e.g. mosquitoes, tsetse flies and the fleas of rodents. However, during epidemics, plague can also be passed directly between infected people when the bacteria proliferate in the lungs (pneumonic plague).

QUESTION 1.2

The military campaigns in Bengal, and the subsequent dislocation of population, spread the bacteria that cause cholera beyond the water courses of regions in which the disease was endemic, to the rest of India and beyond. Although cholera was known in Europe before this time, it reached epidemic levels after it was imported from India along trade routes, arriving in ports such as London where 7000 died in one outbreak in 1832. From Europe it was transported to other colonial territories, reaching North America in 1832 and subsequently spreading into Central and South America. This example illustrates the speed with which an endemic disease in one location can 'globalize' as a consequence of human actions.

QUESTION 1.3

There are many similarities and differences, but here are a few of the most important. Infectious diseases are still currently the major cause of death in developing countries, as they were in pre-industrial Western Europe (indeed until the 1940s). Several infectious diseases of current importance in developing countries were also common in pre-industrial Europe, including plague, TB, cholera, measles and malaria. However, infection has declined in developing countries below the death rates experienced in pre-industrial Europe. For example, even the HIV/AIDS pandemic has not (yet) reached the mortality levels seen during the medieval plagues, when 25% of Europe's population died; smallpox, which caused millions of deaths in the past, has been eradicated worldwide; infant mortality rates in developing countries currently average 65 per 1000 live births — roughly half the rate seen in Scotland as recently as 1900.

QUESTION 1.4

The domestication of livestock and poultry brought their pathogens and parasites into close and prolonged contact with humans; over several thousand years, some of these infectious agents adapted to survive in humans and became the source of important zoonotic diseases (e.g. TB), or adapted still further to become exclusive to human hosts (e.g. smallpox, influenza). In the present day, intensive farming of livestock and poultry is believed to have contributed to the increase in certain food-borne infections (e.g. *Salmonella* and *Escherichia coli* bacteria); the extensive routine administration of antibiotics to food-producing animals may also have contributed to the emergence of antibiotic-resistant bacterial strains.

QUESTION 1.5

(a) In estimating trends in the impact of childhood infections in a population over time, account must be taken of changes in the size of the population 'at risk'. In Scotland (as in other developed nations) the proportion of children is predicted to fall so rapidly over the next 20 years that the *number* of cases of childhood infections is also likely to fall since there are fewer children at risk of contracting them. However, this apparent decline could disguise a rising trend in the *rate* of an infection, that is, an increasing proportion of the dwindling child population could be affected. For example, concerns about the safety of vaccines in the 1990s resulted in falling vaccination take-up for some childhood infections in the UK, followed by rising infection rates of measles in some areas. (A population analysis of these trends appears in Book 6 of this course.)

(b) Some infectious diseases primarily affect children because babies (once breast feeding is over) are 'susceptibles' without the immunity to infectious agents that older people have developed after exposure to the pathogen or a vaccine. Thus, children are the principal population 'at risk' from infections such as measles.

QUESTION 2.1

Koch's second postulate states that the pathogen can be isolated in pure culture on artificial media. Viruses can only multiply within host cells, so Koch would have been unable to isolate the virus using artificial media. (Much later, eggs, and live cells in tissue culture came to be used for growing flu virus, but this was long after Koch's death, and they do not strictly conform to the original postulate.)

QUESTION 2.2

Viral RNA is synthesized in the nucleus of the infected cell. The M-protein and other internal proteins are synthesized on ribosomes in the cytoplasm. The capsid is then assembled in the nucleus. The haemagglutinin and neuraminidase are synthesized on ribosomes on the endoplasmic reticulum. The envelope is derived from the host cell's own plasma membrane.

QUESTION 2.3

Animal strains of influenza act as a reservoir of genes that may recombine with human influenza viruses to produce new strains that can spread rapidly in man. Such pandemic strains frequently produce serious disease with high mortality.

QUESTION 2.4

Cytotoxic T cells and NK cells are able to recognise and destroy virally-infected host cells.

QUESTION 2.5

The virus mutates regularly (antigenic drift); also new strains are occasionally generated by recombination (antigenic shift). Since the immune response is generally specific for a particular strain of virus, new strains are not susceptible to immune defences which have developed against earlier strains.

QUESTION 4.1

Pyogenic bacteria cause infections characterized by the production of pus. Bacteraemia is the medical term for an infection caused by bacteria in the bloodstream. MRSA stands for methicillin-resistant *Staphylococcus aureus*, an antibiotic-resistant strain. A fomite is any inanimate object that acts as a transmission vehicle for an infection, for example, clothing, plastic tubing, surgical instruments and drinking cups.

QUESTION 4.2

Technological advances have kept people alive in hospitals who would formerly have died, and progress in surgery and anaesthesia has enabled hugely complex operations such as organ transplants to be performed. Patients undergoing intensive therapy, such as premature babies, patients with burns or spinal injuries and those recovering from major surgery, can spend weeks or even months in environments with a high risk of infection, such as ICUs and other specialist units. The risk of infection in these locations is principally from invasive life-support procedures involving the insertion of intravenous lines, urinary catheters and respirators, which may have to remain in place for long periods, and in which bacterial and fungal pathogens can grow as adherent biofilms. Additionally, advances in drug treatments for cancer and immunosuppressive drugs to protect organ transplants from rejection, have increased the proportion of patients in hospitals whose immune responses to infection are deficient, and who are at greater risk of becoming infected.

QUESTION 4.3

Infections transmitted to women after childbirth, primarily on the hands of their doctors and midwives, once claimed the lives of up to 30% of women in some European hospitals. In the twentieth century, puerperal fever was eradicated altogether, largely through adherence to hygiene measures by health professionals. Puerperal fever was caused primarily by *Streptococcus pyogenes*, which is now associated with about 5% of surgical site infections in English hospitals (Table 4.1).

QUESTION 4.4

The annual cost of HAIs in terms of staff, tests, treatments, etc., has been estimated at close to £1 billion, so a 30% reduction in incidence would save around £300 million a year. The 14 'extra' days as inpatients for the 100 000 people affected annually with an HAI total 1.4 million bed-days, so a 30% reduction in HAIs could release 420 000 bed-days.

ACKNOWLEDGEMENTS

Grateful acknowledgement is made to the following sources for permission to reproduce material in this book:

Cover

Sleeping sickness parasites (*Trypanosoma brucei*). Coloured scanning electron micrograph of trypanosomes. Jurgen Berger, Max-Planck Institute/Science Photo Library.

Figures

Facing Chapter 1, p. 6:'Girl in White with Cherries', oil on canvas, attributed to Micah Williams, c.1831, Jane Voorhees, Zimmerli Art Museum Rutgers, The State University of New Jersey. Gift of Anna I. Morgan.

Figure 1.1: F. Kuzoe/WHO/TDR; *Figure 1.2*: Andy Crump/WHO/TDR; *Figure 1.3*: Sorsby, A. (1944), *Medicine and Mankind*, Watts and Co Limited; *Figure 1.5*: Bryder, L. (1988) *Below the magic mountain: a social history of tuberculosis in twentieth century Britain*. Reprinted by permission of Oxford University Press; *Figure 1.6*: *Health in Scotland 2000*, Scottish Centre for Infection and Environmental Health. Crown copyright material is reproduced under Class Licence Number CO1W0000065 with permission of the Controller of HMSO and the Queen's Printer for Scotland; *Figure 1.7*: Copyright WHO 2001; *Figure 1.8*: Copyright © Paul Epstein; *Figure 1.9*: reprinted from CDR Weekly, Vol 12, Issue 7, 2002; *Figure 1.10*: 'Mean weekly incidence by gender', Figure 17 in Annual Report 2000, The Weekly Returns Service, Birmingham Research Unit of the Royal College of General Practitioners; *Figure 1.11*: Copyright © WHO; *Figure 1.12*: © World Health Organization 1999: *Figure 1.13*: Williams, B. G. et al. (2002) 'Estimates of world-wide distribution of child deaths from acute respiratory infections', Child Deaths from ARI Review, Infectious Diseases, The Lancet, 2002, Vol 2, reprinted with permission from Elsevier; *Figure 1.14*: courtesy of the CDC/Public Health Image Library, PHIL; *Figure 2.1*: Frederick A. Murphy, Centers for Disease Control and Prevention (CDC); *Figure 2.3*: Noymer, A., and Garenne, M. (2000) 'The 1918 influenza epidemic's effects on sex differentials in mortality in the United States', *Population and Development Review*, Vol 26 (3) 2000, The Population Council; *Figure 2.6*: CNRI/Science Photo Library; *Figure 2.7*: Bammer, T. L. *et al*. (April 28, 2000) 'Influenza virus isolates' reported from WHO, Surveillance for Influenza – United States, Centre for Disease Control and Prevention. *Figure 4.1*: The Wellcome Library, London; *Figure 4.2*: taken from *The Story of St Thomas's* 1106–1947, Faber and Faber Ltd, London 1947 by Charles Graves; *Figure 4.3*: Garry Watson/Science Photo Library; *Figure 4.4*: Dr Rodney M. Donlan and Janice Carr, CDC/NCID: Hospital Infectious Program/Public Health Image Library, PHIL; *Figure 4.5*: 'Surveillance of hospital-acquired bacteraemia, *Sources of hospital-acquired bacteraemia*, Section 2, 1997–2000, Public Health Laboratory Service: *Figure 4.7*: A. Crump, TDR WHO/Science Photo Library; *Figure 4.8*: The Wellcome Library, London.

Every effort has been made to trace all the copyright owners, but if any has been inadvertently overlooked, the publishers will be pleased to make the necessary arrangements at the first opportunity.

INDEX

Note: Entries in **bold** are key terms. Page numbers referring to information that is given only ina figure or caption are printed in *italics*.